HAPPINESS AND CHRISTIAN HOPE

Happiness And Christian Hope

A Phenomenological Analysis

by
William A. Marra, PH.D.

Franciscan Herald Press
1434 West 51st Street
Chicago, Ill. 60609

Library of Congress Cataloging in Publication Data

Marra, William A
Happiness and Christian Hope

1. Happiness. I. Title.
BJ1481.M36   241   79-1119
ISBN 0-8199-0770-7

NIHIL OBSTAT:
  Mark Hegener O. F. M.
  Censor

IMPRIMATUR:
  Msgr. Richard A. Rosemeyer, J.C.D.
  Vicar General, Archdiocese of Chicago

July 31, 1979

Contents

Foreword

Not too long ago, few authors who hoped to reach a large audience would have burdened their work with the word "phenomenological"—even as a subtitle. The word seems to many as hard to spell as it is to pronounce; worse still, it is very hard to define. Its rootword, "phenomenology," has resounded through the philosophical halls of Europe for more than half a century. It has been linked with all the mysteriousness, if not unintelligibility, of the prominent "existentialists," especially Sartre and Heidegger.

I remember the only meeting I had with the French philosopher and dramatist, Gabriel Marcel. He told me that he had renounced the word "phenomenological" to describe his philosophy, even though at first he had had no objection to it. Why? "Because I dislike being linked with those who *call* themselves phenomenologists but whose thought and method are entirely foreign to my own."

But the election of Cardinal Karol Wojtyla as Pope John Paul II bids fair to change many, many things in the world, including even the popularity of the word "phenomenology," but above all the kind of philosophical thinking he means to designate by that word. Now that his books and articles begin to be circulated in various languages, his phenomenological method will become quite clear. The power of his writings and the prestige of his office will ensure widespread favorable acceptance of the method and the word.

Is it possible, though, to give some clear notion of the method in a brief nammer? Yes. At the very beginning of the twentieth century.

1

Edmund Husserl noted that seemingly unbridgeable, contradictory stands on almost every question have been taken by the world's intellectuals. He attributed much of this unhappy situation to the use of the wrong method: too many "hypotheses," to many "speculations," too many "explanations" were mixed in with genuine insights. The result was that truths were offered in the same package as doubtful (and really unnecessary) explanations. He argued that we might achieve far greater unity and consensus in our thinking, even about the deepest and most difficult questions, if we put aside the excess speculations and hypotheses and were content with grasping and understanding "the things themselves."

Now such "things themselves" are the things that are present to our consciousness, whereas their "explanations" may well be absent. They are, therefore, what might be called "appearing" things, as opposed to the recondite things which are supposed to exist but have never been "seen." The Greek word "phenomenon" means precisely the appearing thing, in the sense just specified. Phenomenology for Husserl, its modern founder, and for all his original disciples, is therefore not really mysterious. It is simply the method of thinking which prefers "insight into the given" over any and all explanations and hypotheses. Thus understood, the method is less abstract, less preoccupied with "generic definitions." It is, rather, immersed in the full flavor and differentiations of reality in the concrete. It is thus much closer to common sense and to everyday, lived experience.

There is also, we must admit, a totally different conception of phenomenology; and this too has its roots in Husserl—the so-called "later" Husserl. It was to this conception that a national news-magazine obviously turned, in its article on Pope John Paul II, when it claimed that phenomenology somehow claims to have scientific objectivity because of the peculiar structure or nature of the human mind. This "mysticism" of the mind is at the basis of what has been called "subjective idealism." But Husserl's earlier position was in no way idealistic. His insistence on going to the things themselves has earned for this method of thinking the name "phenomenological realism." This realism, and not the idealism of his later days, is what attracted students of all countries to the University of Göttingen after the publication of Husserl's *Logical Investigations.*

It so happens that among the original disciples of Husserl were Dietrich von Hildebrand and Max Scheler. The latter died, in Germany, in the very year I was born; but I had the great good fortune to meet von Hildebrand in New York, in 1949, at Fordham University, where he was Professor of Philosophy. I studied under him for three years and wrote both my dissertations with him as mentor. I afterward enjoyed the gift of his friendship until his death in 1977. As will be evident, this present book is really an amplification and popularization of his profound thought.

In a true sense, Pope John Paul's "mentor" in phenomenology was Max Scheler—through Scheler's works. The future pope was impressed with Scheler's ethical analyses and sought to bring them into greater harmony with genuine Christian thought. It is apparent, therefore, that much more than the word "phenomenology" is common to von Hildebrand and the Pope. Von Hildebrand received his doctorate under Husserl and was a great friend of Scheler. And during his long philosophical career one of his greatest achievements was the elaboration, through phenomenological analysis, of both a "natural" ethics and a specifically Christian ethics.

We need not dwell further on the phenomenological method. By its fruits we shall be able to judge its efficacy. The general topic of happiness is expecially well suited to test the method. At least the desire for happiness is universal, if not the actual experiencing of happiness is especially well suited to test the method. At least the desire for happiness is universal, if not the actual experiencing of experience. Not the history of philosophy, not the authority and prestige of some renowned method, but *the thing itself* is available to check on the accuracy and adequacy of the analysis.

Introduction

The earthly life of a man stretches between his birth and his death. In that interval a drama unfolds, manysided, with elements of varing depth and intensity. Central to this drama is a restlessness which underlies all earthly experiences. It includes dissatisfaction with present woes, but also with present joys, and a yearning for some undefined, future bliss. This specifically human, specifically earthly situation, with its longings and discontent, is signified by the general phrase "man's quest for happiness."

Because this quest plays such a key role in man's conscious, lived experience, it has inevitably earned the status of a favorite topic of those whose concern is the theory of human life—the philosophers and theologians above all, and now the psychologists and even the political scientists and economists. Theorists have never been lacking to tell us what this quest "really" is, whether it can ever be satisfied, whether it should be encouraged or suppressed by mental discipline, what things can possibly end the quest forever—by fulfilling man's fondest longings—what way of life or what actions ensure fulfillment, and so on.

In ancient times the theories about this quest were clearly named by some such title as "the happy life" or "the nature of happiness." Today, however, because of an unfortunate coincidence of many forces, including a distrust of philosophical "theory" and a corresponding rage for "programs of action," the theory of happiness is concealed beneath such diverse covers as reports in psychoanalysis, case studies in sociology, economic programs of governments, and political ideologies. All of these covers are meant to be theories of "the happy life" or, better, "programs" for the happy life, based on theories only tacitly held.

This book is openly theoretical. It means to ask again the ancient question, still charged with importance and weight: *What* is happiness? Such an investigation is theoretical in the sense that it seeks to understand the nature of happiness; it seeks to dwell on the different kinds of happiness and the relation of happiness to man's life as a whole. The great fault of programs for happiness lies in their ignoring the nature of the very thing they pretend to achieve. Tacitly assuming that "adjustment," or "material welfare," or "success," or some other thing is the happiness that men continue to desire, these programs naively enumerate the steps to be taken to gain the particular good they champion. Hence, despite their sometimes noble intentions, these programs end by being very impractical. Having only a highly restricted, often distorted, partial knowledge of happiness, they cannot possibly be proportioned to the depth and breadth of man's innermost longings.

Ignorance of the truth about happiness and misunderstanding of the nature of happiness not only condemn activist programs to failure, they prevent the opponents of these programs from laying down relevant and effective criticism. A case in point is communism. This is not simply an economic theory or a political ideology, nor is it a religion in any serious sense of the term. It is rather an activist program for earthly happiness. It is based, however, on such a distorted view of man and such a radical misunderstanding of the nature of happiness that it cannot but fail in the very thing it means to achieve: happiness for men on earth. Now the immorality of Communist action—its lies and murders, its brazen justification of violence—have gained for it many opponents. But the majority of these opponents are equipped with only a partial and often distorted view of happiness and are, therefore, ineffective in their opposition. They sometimes weaken and grow fainthearted, for they are attracted by the communist claim of engaging the total man, and they are often seduced into thinking that communism may be, after all, the most profound modern ideology since it seems to satisfy deeply seated metaphysical aspirations. Such faintheartedness could not affect one who has achieved a thorough grasp of happiness in all its forms. The full understanding of the nature of happiness, in fact, will go far in establishing a measure against which all the various activist programs can be evaluated and, if need be, condemned.

The theoretical inquiry into the nature of happiness is further complicated for Americans by the reigning "philosophy," relativism. Still a respectable theory in many universities and, above all, a living, popular attitude that is ubiquitously corrosive, relativism challenges and often defeats—from the start—any serious probe into natures or essences. "If N likes science, then studying science is happiness for him. If R prefers family life, this will be happiness for him." And so on. The question, *What is happiness?* has as many answers, according to relativism, as there are personal likes and preferences. Thus is the truly exciting and momentous theoretical search after the nature of happiness reduced to the recitation, often boring and trivial, of what various individuals happen to like or desire. The result is not a philosophy of happiness, with its critical attempts to grasp causal relations and hierarchical subordination, but an uncritical encyclopedia of pleasant experiences and satisfactions, all implicitly held to be on one level.

The consequences of relativism for lived experience are likewise disastrous. It encourages every individual to elevate his desires and satisfactions to the status of objective absolutes simply because they happen to be *his*. Pampered and made complacent by relativism, the individual is content with the pursuit and occasional enjoyment of one or two goods. For other goods, possibly richer and more meaningful than his own, he has only an uncomprehending shrug and the answer, conveniently supplied by relativism, that different persons are made happy by different goods. If playing golf or reading sensational novels makes him happy, who is to say that such a person is not happy?

All the while, however, even as he flippantly extols his self-elevated absolutes, pressures from deep within his personal being naggingly suggest to him that his absolutes are idols, his desires miserably low, his satisfactions mediocre, incomplete, and often wearisome as soon as they are established in a routine. From the deep comes the muffled but insistent plea: Awake from the sleep of relativism and look about you; lift up your heart, and endeavor to see your true situation as a personal creature in a bewildering, mysterious universe that possibly conceals surprises, delights, and depths that you do not even dream about.

The error of relativism will become progressively manifest throughout this book. Here, however, we may briefly note the following. A man who has elevated a low good into an absolute can be "refuted" simply by showing him a higher good. His error is one of incomplete experience, combined with too great haste in declaring his good to be the last or the best. The cure for relativism, therefore, is a comprehensive survey and accurate evaluation of all the various goods that are given in or through experience.

Still another obstacle to the correct grasp of the nature of happiness is the petrified textbook philosophy which is too often the only proposed alternative to either relativism or complete indifference to theories of any kind. Although it is at least a serious attempt to give a critical, reasoned analysis of happiness, and although it rightly opposes relativism, such a textbook philosophy is but the withered, lifeless branch of what was once the green, living and growing tree of knowledge. Like all dead things it repels most of those who contact it. The few who hold it (perhaps out of misfounded loyalty) uphold a theory of happiness that seems complete and logically harmonious. But such a theory is too remote from the experiences of happiness, too reluctant to reconsider old questions from basically new viewpoints, and too much in love with the notion of a "complete system" to consider any new question from any viewpoint.

There is a great and urgent need in our time not only to reconsider the important questions about happiness which have become obscure and buried, not only to restate eternal verities which have been laboriously discovered by ancient wisdom and so have become basic elements in Western civilization—but also to explore the old questions further, to ask new questions, to confront old conquests with new problems. This book is meant to be the beginning of the answer to this need, for it includes a revival of the momentous question of happiness, a restoration of old truths about happiness, and, above all, a fresh investigation into many aspects of happiness which have been neglected or unstressed.

Chapter 1
The Anatomy of
Happiness

Happiness is a conscious experience. A clear view of happiness in all its varied forms demands a prior explication of the nature of conscious experience itself. In what follows, we propose to divide human consciousness according to two basic principles: "qualitative worth" and "ontological structure." From this will be derived general categories of happiness that will guide all subsequent chapters. The traditional antithesis of "sense" versus "intellectual" happiness will also be considered in this chapter and it will be confronted with the results of our divisions.

Qualitative Worth of Consciousness

The private universe that is our own consciousness is the scene—or better, perhaps, the medium—of experiences which differ in many ways, especially in their worth. The following short list of conscious experiences is set down at random: feelings of hunger, joy, anger, satisfaction, toothaches, melancholy, giddiness, anxiety. It is obvious that some of these—namely, the feelings of joy and satisfaction—are, as such, "welcome." Others, such as anger and anxiety, are, as such, "unwelcome." The terms *positive* and *nega-*

9

tive shall be employed to signify, respectively, the welcome and the unwelcome conscious experiences.

Negative feelings may be likened to "burrs" in our consciousness. They are grasped as somehow opposed to our well-being. They harm us, irritate us, weigh us down. Whether they touch our deepest center—as when we grieve over the death of a dearly loved person—or whether they affect only our periphery—as when we have a headache—they are nevertheless negative, "unwelcome." We may call each such feeling an instance of misery, or simply a negative consciousness. Now since none of these feelings is self-existent, since each is "caused" or somehow "explained" by something besides itself, there will always be an objective correlate to each subjective experience of negative consciousness. We shall employ the term *evil* to signify whatever is responsible on the object side for the negative feeling on the subject side. The term will be given far more precision, of course, as we proceed; for the present, however, it is enough that we have general terms that correspond to large subdivisions of reality.

We have called the qualitative antithesis to negative consciousness "positive consciousness." An experience of this kind, whether involving deep joy or only the pleasant taste of food, is "welcome." Far from being a burr, it is, as such, a friendly presence, which may be likened to a warm glow. The objective correlate of positive consciousness, the thing responsible for the welcome subjective feeling, shall be called a *good*. This term will also be given much more precision as we proceed. In fact, a basic part of this book will be devoted to analysis of the different kinds of goods and the corresponding different kinds of positive consciousness evoked by them.

We must note further that some conscious experiences are qualitatively neutral. That is to say, they neither oppress us nor rejoice us. They are neither burrs nor warm glows. A man may spend some time walking and observing things around him in a casual manner; he may even exert some small effort to effect a change. All the while, he may experience only a neutral consciousness. In one respect, however, even this is positive. His consciousness, by hypothesis, has no burrs and no glows; simply as a functioning consciousness, it has a healthy "tone," a pre-given buoyancy. It is just this buoyancy that, at a later time, can be "weighed down" or "oppressed."

The buoyancy of the neutral consciousness is really an *unformed* positive consciousness—a general state of well-being. It may be compared to the rushing noise that comes from a radio receiver that is tuned to no station. Although this noise is not formed or articulated, it represents something positive, over and above the truly neutral situation of absolute silence. So too, the total lack of consciousness—as is found in a deep sleep—would be truly neutral. The buoyancy of the consciousness that has neither burrs nor glows, on the other hand, is over and above the stillness of this lack of consciousness and thus deserves to be called positive, at least in a secondary sense.

From the qualitative point of view, therefore, we can distinguish four situations: the lack of all consciousness, the unformed positive buoyancy of the awake but otherwise neutral consciousness, the burrs of negative consciousness, and the formed glows of positive consciousness.

Ontological Structure of Consciousness

Conscious experiences may also be divided according to ontological structure. Although a toothache and a sorrow, for example, are both burrs, each occupies a different ontological place in the framework of consciousness. Let us examine the mysterious cavern of human consciousness with a view to distinguishing its principal levels and configurations.

The great structural split among conscious experiences is this: some are *caused* by the agency of material beings acting on the human body and somehow, "invading" human consciousness; others are *motivated*—that is, the person becomes aware of some *object*, distinct from himself. The object is grasped as meaningful. It "acts" on the person, not in any mechanical or material way but through the luminous contact of knowledge—an irreducible, unique contact which can only be called spiritual.

We will now begin to elaborate this all-important difference between caused and motivated conscious experiences. Its full significance will become more and more apparent as we progress.   Let us look first at caused experiences. They can be further subdivided into instincts, states or moods, and sensations.[1] All agree in these basic respects: each is a *conscious result* of some cause that acts on the body and each retains its full character and identity independent of whether the person knows the cause or not. Thus a pain in the chest hurts just as much when we are ignorant of its cause as when we know it. Nor is the pain altered if we find that it is due to a relatively harmless virus and not to some grave damage in the heart. These changes in knowledge make all the difference in our *motivated* conscious experiences, for our fear and worry are replaced by relief; but the pain *as* pain, as a caused conscious experience, retains its exact identity and is experienced with the same intensity and quality as before.

Instincts differ from the other kinds of caused conscious experiences in that they are essentially "incomplete." We experience these instincts as urges, drives, or wants which insist not only on being heard but also on being satisfied. Typical examples are feelings of hunger and thirst. That the body lacks water is simply an objective situation. But something altogether new is the subjective, conscious *feeling* of thirst. This is a "voice" of the body which insists on being heard. We may ignore it for a while but it will not be dismissed. It grows more demanding and insistent. Its very incompleteness gives it a gnawing, dynamic character which is temporarily halted only by temporary completion—by satisfaction or satiety.

What we have called moods or states are, on the other hand, static. Thus the feeling of depression which may come upon us "for no apparent reason" is not an insistent voice, demanding attention and satisfaction. It is rather like a gloomy mist or fog that envelops

---

1. These categories and (generally) the nomenclature follow Dietrich von Hildebrand. See chapter 17 of his *Ethics* (Chicago: Franciscan Herald Press, 1972).

our consciousness. The qualitatively opposite mood of giddiness is another example. Whether it be caused by some hormone or by wine, whether we know the cause or not, the experience is one and the same: a kind of "warm mist" bathes our consciousness.

Sensations, too, are static. We use this term to signify localized bodily feelings, for example, a toothache, the literally warm feeling in the stomach experienced after drinking a cup of hot coffee, the pleasant tingling of the skin when it is lightly stroked, and so on. Such feelings are "affections of the body." They include all *pleasures* and *pains* in the strict sense. Some material cause, acting on the body, is able to excite conscious experiences. Here again, these remain the same, whether or not we are aware of their causes.

Motivated Experiences

All caused conscious experiences, of whatever kind, are, as we have just seen, "immanent." They are conscious reflections of processes enclosed within the bodily organisms. We do not by this mean to deny their possible intensity, or serious impact, or importance. Certainly, because they are experienced by a *man* they attain great significance. But regarded simply as structural, they cannot claim the same importance as motivated conscious experiences.

The latter are specifically *transcendent*. The person is involved not as an organism, absorbing stimuli and then reacting, but as a conscious partner in a dialogue with reality. A completely new level of ontological seriousness is to be found in these transcendent, motivated experiences. The *spirit* of a man is involved. The greatest disaster to truth and clarity arises when one tries to treat these motivated experiences as similar or even identical to caused ones. Thus, while it makes sense to perform research in the hope of finding a pill to overcome feelings of depression, which are caused conscious experiences, it would be nonsensical to look for a "happiness pill" which would rejoice the *spirit* of a man. The spirit will be rejoiced only by objects which are consciously grasped as meaningful.

This all-important world of the spirit, this sphere of motivated experiences, has been called the sphere of "intentionality" or "intentional experiences" by many phenomenologists, following Husserl. Husserl, however, has added certain elements to the concept of intentional experiences which are neither desirable nor necessary. We must guard against interpreting intentional experiences as simply "essential relations" which prescind from existence and are interesting only for epistemological reasons. What makes something an intentional experience is the fact of a meaningful, luminous link between an object and a conscious subject. When, therefore, one *experiences* sorrow, or joy, the experience itself is a concrete existent and the object that motivates it exists or at least is thought to exist. If, later, we reflect on the joy or sorrow, we can discover an intelligible link between our subjective response and the motivating object, and we can see that this link holds true for all cases of the response. Now, of course, we are dealing with essential relations. But this is true of all reflections about types and not just those that involve intentional experiences.

The Meaning of Happiness

On the basis of the above, we can assert that happiness has two fundamental stages. The first is "to be rid of burrs," to go from the negative consciousness that irritates and oppresses us and harms our feeling of well-being to the "zero" of a neutral consciousness, where only the pre-given buoyancy is felt. This kind of happiness, consisting in relief from misery, may be called negative happiness. The second stage is "to be filled with warm glows." We may call this positive happiness. Happiness in the full sense, therefore, will include the absence of burrs and the presence of glows, or instances of positive consciousness.

It is obvious that not all experiences, whether of burrs or glows, are on the same level. We can experience a deep misery or a relatively superficial one. The negative happiness of relief from the one or the other will then vary in depth. We can likewise enjoy a deep positive consciousness or, again, a superficial one. As we noted in the introduction, the only way to realize that one good yields a higher or deeper happiness than another is to have both goods present in experience. The man who knows only the positive consciousness arising, for example, from sports may well be persuaded that "for him, participation in sports constitutes the highest happiness." But let him fall in love. He will then grasp that the love communion yields happiness of a different and far superior rank and quality. He will also see that this in no way diminishes or makes illusory the modest joys offered by sports. Only now these joys are properly evaluated. Their premature elevation to "highest happiness" is canceled and they are seen in their authentic dimensions.

Happiness, then, is not a homogeneous bulk which can be partially in this and partially in that experience—all on one level. There is, instead, a hierarchy of happy experiences in both the negative stage, involving relief from greater and greater misery, and the positive stage, involving the presence of greater and greater glows.

Restricting ourselves for the present to positive happiness, we ask: What makes a positive consciousness "high" or "low"? Given several different experiences of positive consciousness, what elements in the experiences entitle us to rank one above the other?

A long-standing distinction in philosophy, dating at least from Plato, attempts to answer these questions by opposing "sense" happiness to "intellectual" happiness and claiming superiority for the latter. Noble happiness (as opposed to "base pleasures") is said to be strictly an intellectual affair—in fact, simply an activity of the intellect. This distinction, based on a deep-rooted confusion, is worthless. Its widespread acceptance stands in the way of a clear and true understanding of happiness. Let us examine it in greater detail.

A positive consciousness, by definition, involves our *feeling* a welcome "glow" in our consciousness. It is absolutely necessary that the feeling be present; otherwise we shall have not positive but negative happiness, that is, relief from misery, which means a neutral consciousness. Now, as we have seen, a positive consciousness may be either caused or motivated. The pleasant feeling that comes when the skin is stroked is caused; the joy we feel in the long-awaited appearance of a beloved person is motivated—it is an "intentional response." The motivated joy is clearly superior to the caused pleasure. It involves more the center of the person, is richer and more meaningful. Can we say, then, that the feeling of pleasure on the skin belongs to "sense happiness" whereas the joy is a case of "intellectual happiness?" Obviously, if the latter is but another name for motivated happiness, then indeed our distinction between caused and motivated positive consciousness exactly coincides with the traditional distinction between sense and intellectual happiness.

But such is not the case. Motivated happiness for us is a *feeling*, an affection of consciousness—such as is signified by the words "a thrill of delight" or "a leap of joy." The so-called intellectual happiness, on the other hand, is characterized by the absence of any feeling. Thus our joy before the beloved person will be reduced to two components: to the extent that we grasp the beloved as a good and fix our will in an attitude of benevolence, it is intellectual. Just because this intellectual component is stripped of feeling it is claimed to be superior. All feelings are referred to the bodily sphere, which is "low." All "high" experiences are referred to the mind, to the intellectual sphere, and this is exempt from "passions," "emotions"—in short, from feelings.

The great error here centers around the equivocal meaning of the term *feeling*. There are indeed bodily feelings—all of them immanent, caused experiences. We feel our forehead to be hot when it is exposed to a strong light. We feel pain in our finger, hunger in our stomach, thirst in our throat, and so on. So too, on the positive side, we feel a pleasant sensation when the skin is stroked. These feelings indeed may be referred to the "senses"; but there are also "feelings" which are in no way bodily, not immanent, not caused. These are the affections of the spirit, the transcendent intentional responses.[2] Joy before a loved one, enthusiasm for someone's courage, elation over our good fortune—these "emotions" belong as much to the spirit of a man as do knowing and willing. Yet they are, for all that, *emotions*—affections of consciousness that are felt. To be sure, they are, different from bodily feelings even in their quality as feeling. Our joy can in no way be interpreted as "a pleasant sensation," as if

2. Besides the responses there are passive spiritual experiences which consist in our "being affected." See von Hildebrand, *Ethics*, pp. 233–236.

it means some excitation that is felt on some part of the skin. It is rather an excitation and thrill of the spirit.

A theory which confounds bodily feelings with affections of the spirit and lumps these radically different experiences into one vague category, signified by the word "feeling," obviously cannot understand the different levels of happiness. It may rightly see that the spirit of man ranks higher than the body. But when it consigns all "feelings" to the body, it strips the spirit of all affectivity and allows it to have only the placid faculties of mind and will. Thus is prepared the way for the disastrous distinction between high and low happiness: any positive consciousness which is felt is called bodily or sense happiness; consciousness whereby one simply knows a good and *feels nothing* is called intellectual happiness, and is claimed to be superior to the first kind.

From this distinction, moreover, has arisen the phrase "pleasures of the mind," to denote certain alleged joys of the intellectual life. The distinction is also responsible for the scarcely believable insistence by certain thinkers that study, especially philosophical study, is the greatest source of happiness because it satisfies the highest part of man, his mind, by making many truths available to it about the highest realities, for example, God and the soul. In the teeth of all experience to the contrary, these thinkers congratulate themselves on their "higher happiness" and look with bemusement and sometimes pity upon the "deceived" people who enjoy "lower" happiness, *sense happiness*, by reason, say, of their being in love. A man who reads all about this "higher happiness of the mind" can perhaps be forgiven if he concludes that heaven itself is but a higher level of philosophical achievement, a kind of graduate school in philosophy.

To see that his "intellectual happiness" is a confused concept, we have merely to note that knowledge as such need not yield happiness. Whether we experience a motivated happiness or not depends on *what we know*. It does not suffice that we "know truth." The truth we know must be "good news." If it is "bad news," or just an indifferent fact, no joy wells up within us, even though we use our intellect to the utmost. There is, nevertheless, a sense in which knowledge as such may be said to yield positive happiness. We shall discuss this sense in Chapter 4, under the heading of the third kind of "subject-motivated happiness,"

Its existence, however, does not weaken our point that positive happiness is a feeling, for the happiness that sometimes results from knowledge is something over and above the knowledge itself. It is the *feeling* that pervades the spirit as a consequence of a certain intellectual insight into a truth. The theory we dispute says that knowledge *is* the highest happiness, since knowledge involves the exercise of the highest faculty in man. We, on the contrary, say that knowledge often has no link to any happiness at all, and, furthermore, that when it *does* have a link, it is because knowledge *results* in happiness. The disputed theory simply defines happiness as a certain kind of knowledge. We insist that knowledge is always one thing, happiness always another, even when happiness results from knowledge.

This error of identifying the highest happiness with some exercise of the intellect is so widespread and has found so many exponents (especially among ancient and medieval philosophers) that we must try to examine some reasons to account for its wide acceptance. Why, for example, would a worried and overtired student of philosophy, living a lonely and often cheerless existence, hold that he is *really happier* than, say, a man who has fallen in love and married a woman who fully requites his love? Why would Aristotle, who in one place says that genius often makes a man melancholy, hold in another place that the full and perfect exercise of the mind constitutes the highest happiness? Why is it that so few philosophers find the highest happiness in the affective sphere—in love, for example? Why is there almost universal assent that intellectual activity is the supreme principle of all happiness?

It must be that this error derives its strength from at least one truth, distorted and half concealed, but strong enough to give support to the error. We should like to propose, in fact, three such truths that, because they are not fully understood, give comfort to the error.

The first truth is that all genuinely higher happiness is motivated, not caused. There is a real limit to the amount of pleasure or "happiness" which can result from causes that stimulate bodily processes. It follows, then, that higher happiness is possible only when we get to *know* something—a thing that is beautiful or precious or good. Knowledge, therefore, is the great passageway to genuinely higher happiness. All our loves, enthusiasms, joys, and hopes are motivated by an object which is first of all grasped in knowledge. This knowledge of objects need not be the so-called intellectual knowledge, however. Very often, in fact, we rejoice about and love things that are known *through* the senses, for example, friends, a beloved spouse, beauty in nature and art. Still, it is knowledge of some kind which makes possible the entire spiritual life of man, including all the joys and loves which make the heart sing. It becomes somewhat understandable, then, that men should cite knowledge as identical with happiness. They erroneously identify the condition of genuinely high happiness with happiness itself.

The second truth is that a merely neutral consciousness ("negative happiness," in our sense) is much preferable to affections if the latter are *unwanted* affections—hatred, fear, sorrow, anxiety, and so on. Given that a man lives a turbulent life and his consciousness is buffeted by a hundred unwanted affections, such a man will look upon any relief from his affections as a blessed good, a great privilege, a real happiness. Now the intellectual life is admirably fitted to turn a man away from his subjective consciousness, his hopes and fears, loves and sorrows, and toward a world of objects. To him, therefore, the full exercise of his intellect will be a real blessing, for it will enable him to take a vacation from his troubles (so to speak) and to focus his attention on things that are not quite so close to his subjective existence. His yearning for neutral consciousness, therefore—indeed, his well-nigh complete satisfaction with it—enables him to identify happiness with the exercise of the intellect.

A third truth is that life on earth has so many chances for misery, so many inevitable miseries, that no man escapes from great sorrows and bitter disappointments. What is more (as we shall see fully in chapter 8), even the positive joys that life offers are often withheld from a particular man. All this seems to hint to man that his heart can never be at rest while he walks the earth. This hint encourages the man to come to terms of some kind with life. He may reason that if his heart is ever to laugh and rejoice, it will do so in another life, a different world. It becomes, then, a great consolation for suffering man to meditate or at least speculate on this other life, this different world. Thus the life of the mind will be considered a blessing of the highest order, for it will aid its fortunate possessor to see past the miseries of earth and to look for better days in a different life. Of course, the man may renounce all thoughts and hopes of another world. Even so, the life of the mind consoles him in at least a negative, stoical way. It teaches him how to arm himself against the bitter disappointments and great sorrows of earthly life.

In summary, we can say that the exercise of the intellect is erroneously identified with the highest happiness for one or more of these reasons: knowledge, as passageway to precious objects that motivate happiness, is identified with the happiness itself; or the life of the mind really provides a genuine negative happiness, a state of "no feeling" after a previous state of unwanted feelings; or the life of the mind may entertain the possibility, and perhaps the hope, of a better life, or at least it may arm a man to bear the misfortunes of this life with less grief and sorrow.

We may mention a fourth, superficial reason for the error, which may be assumed to operate more with men of little talent than with men of great genius. We mean that pride forces "intellectuals" to think themselves happy, to boast of their happiness as something superior to the joys, say, of marriage and family life. Because they are a bit more gifted than the masses, these "intellectuals" are convinced that they do all things better, live in every way more "intelligently," enjoy all the "higher" things with more sensitivity, than the masses. If it should happen (as it often does) that these men are captives of a slick, superficial intellectualism which starves their spirit and poisons all normal joys, they are forced to identify their wretched life with the "highest happiness," for this is the logical conclusion from their proud assumption that what they do is the best because it is intellectual.

No doubt other reasons may be found to account for the erroneous thesis that the highest happiness does not involve "feeling" but is of a strictly intellectual nature and exists in the "lofty unemotional level of reason." In any case, the consequences of this thesis for philosophy are clear: there is no room for affective feelings; no room for the heart. The senses are seen as bringing us in contact with certain kinds of things that cause pleasant feelings. The mind is seen as pure knower, unperturbed and serene. The will is seen as efficient agent with its decisive yes and no. All height and breadth are granted to the mind, all performance to the will, all feeling to the lowly body. And where is the heart? To what part of man does joy for the presence of a beloved belong? There is no answer—unless the rather pathetic reply that in such cases one experiences an intellectual joy, that is, one *feels nothing.*

When we survey the various kinds of motivated happiness we shall see that each enumerated good is such that it engenders a specific feeling within the heart. To be touched by the beauty of a sunset, to delight in the presence of a friend, to feel love for another pouring out at the very thought of the beloved: these experiences are feelings, emotions, affections. The entire spirit stirs or is stirred. To say that we can love or be delighted without *feeling* love or delight is as nonsensical as to say we can have a toothache and feel nothing.

These feelings, we must repeat, are not bodily, even though they may have some effect on the body. A truly bodily feeling is always *caused:* an agent makes physical contact with some surface of the body and thereby stimulates bodily feelings or sensations. Hot coffee, entering the stomach, yields the *feeling* of warmth; a cool breeze, passing over a perspiring forehead, gives one a pleasant, cool *feeling.* These are bodily feelings. They are caused, not motivated. Also, they are localized in a specific area of the body. The warm feeling is in the stomach, not the foot; the cool, pleasant feeling is on the forehead, not the back. The feelings of the heart, on the contrary, are motivated and not caused. Moreover, they are never localized in any part of the body. Love pervades the *spirit* of the lover. It is not experienced as closer to the foot than to the head. Joy, likewise, is a "feeling" of the spirit and has no spatial relation to any part of the body.

These feelings of the spirit are sometimes so strong that they "spill over" to the body. Our physical heart beats faster when the spirit is affected with a strong love or delight. But this bodily aftereffect is strictly secondary. The spirit must first *know* some object; it must then respond with an affection. Only after these two things have been accomplished will the bodily aftereffect be possible. Motivated feelings, because they come from the spirit's response to what it knows, envelop the body; they can even be said to overwhelm the body. In this, they are just the opposite of caused feelings, which, being bodily to start with, invade the spirit's domain and caress it with warm or cold touches, as it were.

Chapter 2
Negative Happiness:
The Relief from Misery

Are there affections of heart that we should prefer to be without? Are there experiences we dread, which we pray may never befall us? Do we find before or within us things which need simply become absent for us to consider ourselves happy? To all this the answer is an emphatic yes. In this chapter we wish to survey the different kinds of misery, the "burrs" of consciousness which, when removed, lift us to a neutral consciousness that we rightly denominate as bliss. Not all, or even the greatest, miseries of life will be discussed here. We reserve Chapter 8 for a fuller, more methodical treatment of the evils of life, considered as a whole. Here we are concerned with establishing categories of evil.

Three broad areas of misery may be distinguished. The first, which we shall call "direct miseries," are those that come from evils which attack or threaten the person himself. The second, called "miseries of the hearth," are those that arise from evils that attack the person through his private circle—his "hearth." The third, "miseries of society," are due to evils that affect the person insofar as he is a member of the community of men spread over the world.

Direct Miseries

A man has only to exist and he will be subject to certain evils that directly afflict him. The most obvious pertain to the immanent sphere and operate through the body. Merely to have an urge or drive—an instinct—which is not satisfied is already a burr. Thus heading the list of direct miseries by reason of their universal and clearly grasped agency are those pains which arrive when the most primitive and basic needs of man's bodily health are not satisfied. The objective lack in the body—whether of food, drink, or sleep— causes the negative consciousness, the pangs and burrs and bodily heaviness that oppress so many and, potentially, can oppress all men.

To satisfy bodily needs requires work. This is not always painful and in fact can sometimes be enjoyable. Prolonged and excessive work, however, with little respite—as is the lot of most mankind— causes a general weariness which is obviously negative. Thus, considered merely as a living being, man goes from the misery of unsatisfied needs to the misery of excessive labor that tries to satisfy the needs. It is especially here that technology can come to man's help, by reducing the intensity and duration of the labor needed to sustain life.

Our survey of direct evils must also include the enemies to bodily well-being—the evils that attack man from the outside and inflict pain and suffering on him: wounds of all kinds, diseases that bring with them fever and pain, and so on.

These caused miseries are bad enough. They are so immediate and compelling that a man who is afflicted with them is easily led to believe that happiness means simply the cessation of bodily miseries: the end of hunger, the absence of pain, the cure of sickness, the unburdening of his body from oppressive labors. But let a man actually be rid of these immanent miseries and he will find not the expected neutral consciousness, but miseries of a different kind, pertaining to his spirit. These miseries seemed not important or severe as long as he was struggling against the miseries of the body. But now they come to the foreground of consciousness and begin to gnaw and oppress.

What are these miseries of the spirit, these transcendent motivated burrs? There is, first of all, loneliness. This has a relative and an absolute form. A solitary man can look at others who have friends and spouses and envy them: how lonely he is relative to them. There is no person in his life to listen to him with interest and share his experiences. He has no one to rejoice with him in his hopes and calm him in his fears. What would he not give for another person, another world of self-consciousness to meet his own! They could talk together, share emotions of joy and sorrow, plan together. But he is lonely—there *are* no other persons. He is seen and known only by the impersonal sun, the impersonal earth. Friendly animals come near him and are gentle, but they neither understand nor answer him. They too, in fact, seem stranded.

Such are some of the miseries of relative loneliness. The suffering of the lonely man is so often unendurable that he seeks relief by suicide. Indeed, most statistical studies cite loneliness as the greatest reason for suicide. We may infer from this the great suffering of the lonely man. Why else would a man take so desperate a step as suicide, fraught with so many uncertainties and moral horrors, except that he is gripped by something which to him is even more horrendous, namely, the despair of loneliness?

Compared to the man of relative loneliness, persons who have friends and spouses seem secure and fortunate in their communion. True, the latter escape the relative loneliness of the solitary man, but they are liable to "absolute loneliness," which can come to any person, no matter how generously endowed with friends and loved ones. It brings a deep sense of estrangement which, although not sharply painful, saddens the spirit, perplexes it, and even opens it to the *anxiety* that present-day existentialism stresses so much.

The lonely man, in this absolute sense, is the one who has discovered himself. He was not lonely so long as he had no explicit self-consciousness, so long as his personality was merged with the environment. The day came, however, when he began to look at himself as in a mirror, except that he looked at his conscious self, his inner, subjective existence. How mysterious his person seems to him now; and how strange and foreign, perhaps hostile and unfriendly, seems the world. He experiences great emotions within himself. He is awed by the immensity of the world, frightened by its great silences, moved to tears by its beauties, saddened by its headlong rush into future times. He sees himself as one stranded on a place of great mystery. A hundred objects and aspects of the world parade before his sight; a hundred different responses are given by himself to what he knows. But underlying all these activities of consciousness is the somber, sustained realization: *he is all alone.*

Loneliness carries with it a sadness akin to self-pity. The lonely man feels rejected, unwanted, and even ignored by a universe which displays an impersonal coldness toward his tender, subjective existence. This form of loneliness touches a stratum of personal consciousness which cannot be reached by spouse or friends, no matter how intimate. It seeks what we may call a "metaphysical relief." We shall return to this classical desire of man in chapter 6, when we discuss the relationship of God to happiness.

Another misery of the spirit is frustrated longing or desire. To have before us a glittering good, to desire it ardently, and to know with increasing certainty that we can never possess it—this is a sharp burr, a cutting sorrow. This too shall be treated more fully in a subsequent chapter. Here it is necessary only to mention it.

Several additional direct miseries of the spirit need to be listed: disgust with self over moral failure, cares and worries, and the whole class of miseries which result from "poison darts" directed to us by other people. The typical or representative manifestations of this latter class are to be blamed and criticized in a certain way, to be insulted, to be the recipient of ill will and arrogant remarks, and—above all—to be hated. In all these cases we feel as if another person's malice had been compressed into a slender dart and driven into our consciousness. The misery it creates there will depend, of course, on the nature of the "poison" and the intention of the other person, and also on our general attitude.

Miseries of the Hearth

The "hearth" is, *par excellence*, the locus of the community of love. Only intimates gather here, united by bonds of affection and loyalty. As we shall see, this close circle of persons who are united by love is the source of the deepest earthly happiness. But it also has a negative side. A lover of whatever kind—parent, friend, spouse, or child—is like a man ascending a perilous slope. Every foot gained is the source of a new delight to him, but it makes a fall more terrible. At last a kind of summit may be reached, and delight is full. But should he fall, a far greater injury will result than if he had never begun to climb. So, too, the man who loves a little stands to lose but little. The man who loves more is open to more delight but open, too, to more agony.

Love of whatever kind has two basic "intentions" or inner tensions, namely, union and benevolence.[1] Each entails a specific misery when it is frustrated.

Let us look first at the intention of union. It is the lover's longing, and his delight, to be *one* with the loved one. If the desired union is impossible for one reason or another, the lover undergoes a typical "misery of the hearth."

How is the intention of union frustrated? First of all, union may never begin. In the case of spousal love between the sexes, the failure of requital frustrates from the start the union desired by the lover. So long as the loved one fails to return love for love, of the same kind and intensity, the union is not accomplished. Nothing can substitute for this requital—not nearness in space, not even bodily nearness in sex. Something analogous to this unrequited spousal love can be found in parental and filial love. It is never, as such, so bitter, however, for only in spousal love is the *complete* heart offered.

Given that a love communion (of whatever kind) exists, so that the persons are united in spirit by mutual love, and given that they enjoy life together, this union may be temporarily frustrated by absence in space. With this comes misery. Unhappy hours, anxious and lonely, are spent when wives are separated from their husbands and parents from their children. This is always the case during a war and, tragically, after most wars, when whole populations are uprooted and forced to separate and when prisoners are not returned.

---

1. See von Hildebrand, *In Defense of Purity* (Chicago: Franciscan Herald Press, 1970).

The union of life together is permanently and abruptly fractured by death. The death of loves ones, even the fear of their death, is a deep and overriding evil which motivates such burrs in the lover's consciousness as can scarcely be endured. In chapter 8 we shall discuss this misery at length, when we treat of the enemies of earthly happiness.

The intention of benevolence is the second sinew of love. The lover, to the extent that he loves, is completely free from egoism and self-interest. His concern is rather for the *beloved*, for her happiness and well-being. This intention itself has two sides: to ward off evils that militate against the loved one's happiness and to heap positive goods on the loved one to increase her joy. The latter has hardly a chance of being accomplished to the degree every lover wants. He is limited in many ways and so prevented from bestowing a fraction of the good he desires to bestow. No spouse thinks his gift adequate, no parent thinks he has done enough for his child's happiness. Moreover, when it comes to preventing misery, those who love are even more limited and inadequate. Too often they are forced to look on helplessly as the loved one is made wretched and unhappy. To see misery in a loved one is to *be* miserable oneself.

A special instance of misery, possible only in the communion of love, is summed up by the phrase "sickness of heart." It refers to the tearing pain a person feels when he sees that his loved one is the agent of moral evil. A loving son, who learns of his father's unfaithfulness in marriage, is sick of heart if he knows this. A loving parent who discovers his child to be a thief (or worse) is likewise sick of heart.

The most classical type of heart-sickness comes when a person must live with the knowledge that his or her spouse is engaged in a moral evil, especially adultery. Othello's response is not made less genuine by the fact that Desdemona was really innocent. For had Desdemona been what he thought she was, the very same responses would have poured from him in all their pathos and bellowing torment.

> But there, where I have garner'd up my heart,
> Where either I must live or bear no life,

The fountain from the which my current runs
Or else dries up; to be discarded thence!
Or keep it as a cistern for foul toads
To knot and gender in!

True, the torment of an Othello is a combination of sickness of heart over the supposed moral evil of his once beloved spouse and anger because he believes he has been cuckolded. We can, however, distinguish the role played by each motive and appreciate how painful are the welts of a man who "catches" his precious wife, his once exalted jewel, degraded in adultery.

Miseries of Society

An egoist, a man who is filled with himself, has only a single point of concern: his own well-being. He is therefore insulated from the evils that affect other men. To the extent that a man is not an egoist, however, he becomes aware of invisible channels which carry the miseries of humanity into his own heart. Let him walk through certain buildings (prisons, hospitals, etc), let him visit certain places (battlefields, refugee camps), let him only read the papers for a week, and he will say with Macbeth: "I have supped full of horrors!"

Humanity is a community wherein most of the members most of the time are afflicted with every variety of evil, resulting in every kind of agony and heartache. Let us think of the vast numbers who are subject to famine or near-famine, sickness, and other evils related to the immanent bodily sphere. Let us think of all the families that are separated by inner discord or external compulsion. Add to this all the evils that befall soldiers and civilians in war. Add also the evils inflicted on others by criminals, corrupt officials, and racketeers who victimize the weak.

To know this is to suffer. Many burrs twist in our consciousness when we reflect on the miseries of others. These include our movements of sympathy and pity (which cost us so much!) and our responses of outrage and indignation, and concern to help. If we decide to help others, the efforts we expend are additional burrs.

Summary

When we reflect on these miseries, whether direct, or of the hearth, or of society, we appreciate how one very valid and profound meaning of happiness is this: "That all these ills should depart!" To be happy is to have the ulcers of misery one by one removed, until we are conscious of—nothing! Since the word "happiness" refers generally to something we desire, it is evident that this relief from misery, because it is desired above all else by every man, deserves the name of happiness. *Not to suffer* the weariness of the limbs, *to be free* at last from sharp pains in the body, to have worry and anxiety *erased* from consciousness, *to have no occasion* to pity others and be concerned with their troubles, *to be rid of* sickness of heart and despair before the onslaughts of time: let these things be! Let each release come and a man shall deem himself blessed.

This first meaning of happiness, as relief from misery, is important and valid. To pass lightly over misery, to act as if the sorrows of life are but the inventions of a soured pessimist, is to misunderstand happiness in every sense. Many an ethics book, many a book on the philosophy of history, many a cheerful word on the meaning of life have mocked ethics, history, and life with their stupid blindness to the fact of evil and misery. But to say that relief from misery is a mighty good, an important *desideratum*, is not to say it is the *only* meaning of happiness. Schopenhauer, so keenly alive to life's miseries, thought that relief from them was happiness enough. Though he knew of positive pleasures and joys, he was so preoccupied with the disproportionate misery their absence would cause that he preferred to see happiness as the neutral consciousness, cleared of all turbulence and sorrow, but likewise free of any effervescent delight.

Schopenhauer's error will be made apparent when we survey positive happiness. In chapter 9 we shall return to Schopenhauer and show that his philosophy is but a clearly and frankly stated theory of life which is shared by all pagan ethics, but is implied rather than openly stated, as if the naked assertion of life's miseries would be too unbearable to men who have committed themselves to making the best of this life since they know of no other.

Although Schopenhauer is the first Western philosopher of renown to teach that happiness is negative, since it means freedom from all the great miseries of existence, he was preceded in this doctrine by the beliefs of the Oriental religions, especially Buddhism. When we think of the great multitudes who subscribe to this and to similar religions, we may safely estimate that over half the people of the world mean only one thing when they think about happiness, namely, relief from all pain and sorrow, from all frustrated stirrings—from misery in all its forms.

Chapter 3
Positive Happiness

We have noted that to enjoy "positive happiness" means to have within oneself a welcome, positive consciousness. The experience is felt now as a pleasure, now as a warm glow, now as a thrill or delight. Our consciousness stirs or is stirred in a positive way. The inner experience also has an outer side; that is to say, it is externalized through facial expressions and thus made an object of perception by others. We can easily recognize positive happiness, therefore, if we refer to just these external expressions.

Let us think of the face of a man expressing sorrow, then relief from sorrow, then delight. In the first instance, the weight of sorrow presses to his brow, his eyes are dulled or pained; his mouth and lips and jaw hint that he is ready to cry. Remove the reason for his sorrow, and give him relief from every pain and misery, and his face will assume a blank expression. He will then enjoy what we have termed "negative happiness." His neutral state of consiousness will be evident in the relaxed features of his face. But now give him reason to rejoice, now fill his heart with some instance of positive consciousness, and his face lights up, his eyes glitter. As if a new principle had entered him, he is transformed by this positive happiness, though it be but a minute. For that minute, at least, his spirit is filled with inrushing joy; a thrill of delight surges through him. This is an instance of positive happiness.

We must now analyze the different kinds of positive conscious-

33

ness, for their proper ordering and understanding will give us the true nature of happiness. A positive consciousness that is caused or immanent is relatively simple to understand, and we will treat this kind first. We will then discuss the very different kinds of motivated positive consciousness. These motivated, transcendent experiences are much more complex and varied.

A caused positive consciousness is always the result of a physical contact between the human body and some stimulating agent. When conditions are right, the latter excites pleasant sensations which slip into our consciousness. It is a matter of everyday experience, empirical fact, that some objects have this power of pleasant excitation whereas others do not. However, the exact link between the mechanical, bodily stimulus and the *subjective feeling* remains, like consciousness itself, a great mystery. But it is enough for our theory of happiness that we recognize the fact that bodily changes result in conscious experiences, even though the process is not intelligible to us.

Material objects that have certain flavors or odors are capable of producing a caused positive consciousness. Thus tasty foods and beverages undeniably yield "pleasures of the palate." Perfumes, salty air, and pine-scented breezes excite a specific pleasure in us.

The greatest channel of caused pleasures, however, is neither taste nor smell, but *touch*. The many surfaces of our skin (some much more than others) are sensitive to stimulations which yield caused pleasures. The specific *bodily pleasures* of sex—as opposed to the concomitant delights of the spirit—are excellent examples of caused pleasures that are given through touch.

It is obvious that not all experiences that originate in touch are pleasurable. Some are neutral, for example, the sensations of moderate heat and cold and the feeling of certain textures—rough, smooth, and the like. Some are painful. Any stimulating cause that exceeds certain limits by that very fact yields a negative feeling, a burr.

Interestingly, the senses of sight and hearing are liable only to caused pain, not to caused pleasure. A light that is too strong and a sharp or excessively loud sound, can pain us in a bodily way. Our eyes feel as if stabbed, our ears and head feel crushed. These are negative feelings and are rooted, perhaps surprisingly, in touch, which seems to be the ubiquitous sense. There is, however, no corresponding positive pleasure of the eye or ear. If we look upon a beautiful object, we cannot truly say that our eyes are pleased, as if the light rays, instead of stabbing the eyes and causing them pain, caress and soothe them. So, too, a pleasing melody or a beautiful song are not pleasures *for the ear* in the same way that the sharp sounds are pains for the ear. On the contrary, the positive consciousness that comes from sight or hearing is always *motivated.* The *object* of sight or hearing, when *known*, can rejoice or delight us.

Aristotle believed that the proper functioning of any faculty is "accompanied by pleasure." Especially with respect to the faculties of sensation, he would have been closer to the truth had he asserted only the converse, namely, that the improper functioning is accompanied by pain. The proper functioning, on the other hand, is as such neutral. One *feels* no pleasure in simply looking at a commonplace building or listening to casual sounds. At times, it is true, even the normal functioning of any faculty yields us a "vital pleasure"; we feel a "zest" in simply seeing, breathing, hearing, and so on. But this is by no means the rule. The danger of following Aristotle in this is that we will come to think of neutral feelings as "pleasures," resulting from proper activity, or we will regard the occasional instances of zestful activity as if they are typical examples of pleasure. Meanwhile, we will overlook or minimize the formed, positive pleasures that are rooted in touch, taste, and smell.

Motivated Positive Consciousness

To the sphere of motivated positive consciousness belong all the delights and joys, all the "glows" of experience, that remain after the caused pleasures have been counted. Despite many variations, all states of motivated positive consciousness agree in one basic respect: we are somehow conscious of a meaningful being and *because of this being, insofar as it is known,* we experience a positive, a welcome glow.

We have already adopted a terminology whereby the objective correlate to a positive experience shall be called a "good." Thus, for a motivated positive consciousness to exist, it is necessary that we somehow know a good. This good, as known, will truly *form* the subjective consciousness that is engendered by it. Thus—as a general rule—the quality, depth, and intensity of any motivated positive consciousness will depend on the nature of the good that engenders it. It follows that great differences among the goods of the universe will be reflected in proportionately great differences among experienced happiness.

Many different kinds of goods have been noticed and elaborated in philosophy. In fact, our distinction between caused and motivated positive consciousness implies a distinction among goods that is based on their relation to the different structures of consciousness. Philosophers have distinguished between goods of the body and goods of the soul, or between temporal and eternal goods, or between goods that are easy and hard to procure. Some moderns even distinguish between social and antisocial goods. Now it is almost always the case that a given distinction is accurate—it really points out two kinds of things that might be confused. Still, the serious question about a distinction is this: Is the distinction important? Does it get to the root differences of things? Or does it merely elaborate a superficial difference, all the while allowing profound differences to go unnoticed?

One of the greatest distinctions between goods ever elaborated in philosophy must be credited to Dietrich von Hildebrand. In all his works, but especially in *Ethics*, he has used this distinction, between "value" and "subjectively—satisfying goods," to effect an immense clarification of the nature of man and of the universe that confronts man.

Von Hildebrand discovered that the great split between "goods" is based not on any body–soul or time–eternity dichotomy, but rather on this basic point: some things are "good," that is, they motivate joy, desires, enthusiasm, etc., because they are grasped by me as capable of satisfying something within me, whereas other things are "good" because they possess an intrinsic importance or splendor *prior to* and *independent of* any delight or positive consciousness they may engender in me. He calls the first goods "subjectively satisfying"; the others, which are already or intrinsically important, he calls "goods of value" or simple "values."

Goods of either kind, of course, afford us delight or positive consciousness. In fact, it is on this account that we called them goods in the first place. But if we analyze the exact nature of the delight that each affords us, we realize that in the case of the subjectively satisfying, the delight or satisfaction is prime. The good is measured by its ability to satisfy some subjective center in us. In the case of value, however, the delight is both psychologically and ontologically secondary. If I confront a good of value—a beautiful landscape, for example, or even better a beloved friend—I must psychologically attend to the beauty or the friend and not to the delight that each shall afford me. My whole interest must be focused *on* the value and *away* from any link to myself.

Moreover, the joy that comes to me as I drink in the beauty of the scene, or move in the presence of the beloved friend, is a joy that is ontologically dependent on the value itself. This kind of joy is possible only because it is motivated by something serious and intrinsically important, something detached from my ego's self-affirmation. In the presence of values, whether great ones, such as beloved friends and beautiful scenes, or modest ones, such as grace and agility in an athlete, I am instantly aware that I am being treated to a "banquet" and that all the "work" is done by the object. I have only to receive. The full warmth and splendor and special flavor of each value streams into me and gives me the special delight and attractiveness of the object, independent of any of my subjective satisfactions.

Guided by this distinction of von Hildebrand, we propose to use it in our theory of happiness and to broaden it and expand upon it in certain directions. We will therefore divide goods according to this principle of division: the exact role of the personal *subject* as opposed to that of the *object* in constituting the goodness of a being. This principle of division will yield four major classes of good, the first three of which were seen and elaborated more or less in detail by von Hildebrand. The fourth major class (which will be treated in the next chapter) represents a new subdivision of goods and our analysis of it will represent an addition to von Hildebrand's value theory.

The first class of good is exemplified in situations where the subject is completely at rest, so that the full quality and form of the subjective experience is explicable in terms of the object alone. If the object is a neutral fact, the subject has no formed response. If the object is a disvalue, however, something that ought not to be (e.g. the torture of a child by a member of the secret police in a totalitarian state), the subject perceives the true configuration of this disvalue and responds accordingly—with horror and indignation. This, of course, is an example of evil. But since it is the exact reverse of the good of this first class, it throws the latter into relief. If the object is a good of value, something intrinsically precious and important (e.g. the heroism of someone who rescues a drowning man or the lovable quality of some person), the subject perceives this good and responds solely on account of it.

In this first situation, where we as conscious subjects contact a good of value, it is as if we attend a spiritual banquet. All the flavor and charm and attractiveness are on the object side. We have only to receive—in reverence and awe. The polar antithesis to this banquet situation occurs when we place a subjective attitude between ourselves and the object and distort it so much as to reverse its objective sign. The result is a second class of goods, fully opposed to the first. In this "moral distortion" it is as if a lens, ground and polished by our wickedness, inverts values and disvalues. It is thus the subject, and not in any way the object, that is responsible for the "goodness" of the object. Let us look at the following examples.

An acquaintance of ours, at the peak of prosperity, suffers a disastrous reverse in business and is forced to give up his beautiful home and to adopt a much lower standard of living. We, hearing about this, rejoice. Why? Does the *object* call for joy? Is it something of value, of positive importance in itself, that another man be brought down in the world? Not at all. If this were the first situation, wherein the subject is completely at rest, it would bring forth our concern for the man's trouble. But it is not so. We have placed the lens of our *envy* between the object and ourselves. So it is that the object is "good." It glitters—not with the autonomous brilliance of value but with the derived light reflected from our envy.

Again, we own a thriving business. One of our clerks greatly overcharges an unsuspecting customer of modest means. Learning of this, we are pleased; the overcharge will result in more profit for us. Here the lens of *greed* distorts the objective situation and makes a "good"—something positive and attractive—over what is objectively a disvalue—something negative, which ought not to be.

Both examples of the second class of goods are instances of what von Hildebrand calls "subjectively satisfying goods." The first distortion stems from the subjective center of pride, the other from the center of concupiscence. In both instances the subjective centers distort being and invert its authentic sign. It is the great privilege of man, as he walks through time, to grasp things as they are, things of value in their axiological splendor and of disvalue in their ugliness and negativity. Correspondingly, the horrendous capacity in man is that he can wickedly invert things through the distorting, self-fashioned lens of his pride and concupiscence. These distortions often occur without being fully willed by the person. His pride and concupiscence are almost "natural" to him. They steadily and effortlessly grow, while their distorting lenses are constantly refined.

A third class of good, also isolated by von Hildebrand, can be called "legitimate subjectively related goods." They differ from values in that their goodness is not autonomous but derived. They differ from the second class of good because they imply no distortion of objective worth by the subject, even though they are related to the subject. To this class belong all the goods which can cause immanent pleasures: cooling breezes, delicious foods, and so on.

We must note the following about these goods of the body: although, in their "operation," they yield a caused positive consciousness, they can also be objects of certain motivated consciousnesses which must be considered positive. Thus the desire for and then the expectation of a flavorful meal is a motivated experience. It is a glow of the spirit. The actual enjoyment of the meal, however, is an immanent experience, yielding the caused pleasure of the palate which we have already discussed. Finally, after the meal has been enjoyed, we experience an overall feeling of satisfaction and well-being, which again is a motivated consciousness and thus an affection of the spirit.

We have called goods of this kind "subjectively related goods." By this we mean to stress that their goodness, their glitter before our consciousness, is essentially dependent upon ourselves. They are positively important—as opposed to being neutral—because they can gratify some subjective center, whether of comfort or pleasure. Von Hildebrand has taken great pains to show the radical difference between the autonomous, underived good of values on the one hand and, on the other, both the morally distorted goods, which depend on the subjective centers of pride and concupiscence, and the legitimate goods (just discussed), which are related to an innocent subjective center.

The consequences of this distinction for a theory of happiness are of the first importance. The positive consciousness that is motivated by values is of a quality distinct in every essential from the positive consciousness that is yielded by subjectively satisfying goods, whether distorted or innocent. When we take up in detail the "banquet happiness" due to values, we shall see the vast distance between the two kinds of happiness, a difference which could almost be signified by the antithesis "heaven" and "hell."

Chapter 4
The Role of Subjectivity

The threefold distinction of goods listed in the previous chapter, is based on the principle of division which asks whether the goodness of the being is rooted fully in the object or, instead, is due to either a subjective distortion or a legitimate subjective relation. We now want to consider a fourth class of goods which we shall call "goods of subjectivity." Although this class was not treated by von Hildebrand, our elaboration represents an organic development of von Hildebrand's theory of good. Especially for the understanding of happiness is this fourth class of goods important.

In general, a good of subjectivity involves the fact that the very *being of the self*, in one or another actualization, is the object of a motivated positive consciousness. Thus the happiness that comes from goods of this kind involves the self in a special way. The difference between this self-involvement and all the other already-treated forms of subjective relations will soon be manifest.

Goods of subjectivity fall into two large classes, active and passive. In the former, "ourself as active" is the motivating object of a positive consciousness. In the latter, it is "ourself as recipient." Goods of active subjectivity yield what we shall call a "subject-motivated happiness"; goods of passive subjectivity yield what we shall call a "self-involved joy or happiness."

41

Active Subjectivity

Any just meditation on the times during which we considered ourselves "happy" would unfailingly include the following: our joy in having *achieved* something; the delight of having a long-cherished desire realized in an electrifying *now*; and, again, the elation that attends our *knowing* something. All three examples belong to the class of goods which we have termed "goods of active subjectivity." Some part of our inner self provides the very reason and motive for our joy. Experiences of this kind possess a kind of transcendent immanence. They are in no way mere actualizations of bodily processes, as are all strictly immanent experiences of pain, giddiness, and the like. On the contrary, they are intentional, motivated experiences. And yet the motive is "enclosed" within the self. The result is what we might call a "spiritual zest," rooted in the specific activity of the spirit.

Achievement

The positive consciousness—the joy or the "feeling good"—which results from achievement is brought into focus if we consider the following example. A man accepts two fresh fish from his neighbor with polite gratitude. If he enjoys fish he will be happy, because he now has some fish to eat. But if he does not care for fish, the possession of the fish is a matter of indifference to him. If he feels anything pleasant at all, it is because of his neighbor's generosity and not because of the fish. Now the same man awakens early the next morning and goes on a fishing trip of his own. The weather is foul; wading up-and downstream is tiring and often painful, because of sharp rocks, deep holes, and so forth; but the man catches two fish after a few hours. He is happy. He looks at his catch and says to himself: I have caught these! Plainly, his happiness is motivated by the good of active subjectivity. What pleases him is not the fish but the fact that he has achieved something, however trivial, after a long effort. The same man would be less pleased if he could catch two similar fish every day by simply putting his line into a well-stocked lake for a minute. He would be completely indifferent, moreover, if he perceived that all the people around him were achieving the same thing.

Achievement as such, considered as a source of happiness, has several interesting properties. Its ability to please me rests on my successfully metting a *challenge*. I must feel that I have done something that is not easily done. To climb a dangerous mountain or to cut through uncharted jungles is to achieve something rare, and it is this which pleases me. My joy does not depend on another's appreciation of my success. Insofar as simple achievement is at stake, I am pleased because I know how well I have performed. Any added joy that results from the knowledge that others have of me would fall under the separate category "fame" (as we shall see in later chapters).

Joy over achievement, moreover, despite its basis of subjectivity, has a link with the specific objective thing that I accomplish at any given time. The link is twofold. In one way, my joy varies with the objective difficulty of the thing; in another way, with the objective importance of the thing achieved. Both ways need not operate together. In fact, men may be profoundly distinguished as they stress the one or the other. We may call the first way "acrobatic achievement" and the second "benefactor achievement."

A person who is interested only in acrobatic achievement asks but one question: How difficult is the task? The more difficult, the more it pleases him. Whether the task has the form of a man-made contest, in which difficult challenges are carefully formulated, or whether it is concerned with a natural challenge is of no importance. Neither does he care if utilitarian benefits are present in one instance and absent in another. His sole measure is difficulty, artificial or natural; his sole scale of pleasure is the greatness of the difficulty overcome, whether with beneficial or useless results. Thus a man who is ruled solely by this motive would get more happiness from staying under water for a very long time than in swimming a mile across a choppy lake, provided only he thought the former more difficult, He would also prefer doing a difficult feat in athletics, say

150 push-ups, to achieving a more useful but easier task, such as surveying rough terrain.

Acrobatic achievement carries with it two secondary forms of positive consciousness. The first is the satisfaction we feel in the mere fulfillment of any tension. A task or feat is proposed—and it is done. We run to catch a bus and we just succeed. We feel satisfied, even though missing the bus would have meant no inconvenience at all. The second form is the joy that comes with ability. Once we have mastered a difficult process, we perform it with a facility that yields a positive satisfaction.

The joy that comes from benefactor achievement, although based on an active subjectivity, varies according to the objective rank of the deed. The worth and glory of the object will reflect back on the achievement and give the latter its proportionate worth. A person will feel greater pleasure, therefore, in realizing that he has established peace between formerly hostile people than in knowing he has repaired a leaking roof that had resisted previous attempts by experts and that is considered dangerous to climb. To appreciate how much the happiness that is based on subjectivity contributes to the total effect, we must separate the man's joy in personal achievement from his joy over the fact that something good has happened. This latter joy, a "value response" in the strict sense (see chapter 5), can be present when someone else establishes peace or repairs the roof. Thus, though a man had nothing to do with it, he can rejoice because peace has come or because the leak has been stopped. The specific pleasure of benefactor achievement, on the contrary, springs from the man's knowledge that he himself had something to do with bringing this good about. It is a joy all its own, a joy rooted in achievement. Nevertheless, as we have seen, its quality and depth are proportionate to the objective good achieved.

A physician, surveying his long years of service, may experience a deep joy of benefactor achievement, motivated by his knowledge that he has been responsible for certain good things. Nor can we call him vainglorious or proud for feeling thus. Indeed, he experiences this joy of benefactor achievement only because he understands, as he surveys the good things done by him, that he has been *privileged* to have been selected as a worker for the good things. He sees himself as an actor in an enterprise that is truly noble and beneficial. With this attitude he undertook the task in the first place, and it is the same attitude which runs through his joy of achievement in a job well done.

The "Now" of Fulfilled Desire

A second kind of subject-motivated positive happiness is evident when a desire, cherished for a long time, is at last fulfilled. Here again, the subject-motivated happiness is likely to be found mixed with an object-motivated joy. The latter results because the object itself is precious or attractive; to possess it, consequently, bestows a certain amount of joy on the person. This joy is fully objective grounded on the goodness of the object. Furthermore, to account for this joy, we need not postulate a prior desire or longing on the part of the rejoicing person. It is enough that he now possesses an attractive or precious thing. The subject-motivated joy, however, which is what concerns us now, depends precisely on a prior longing. It is motivated by the realization of an electrifying *now*—when some long-desired object is at last possessed.

Let us analyze this datum of desire. I look about me and perceive something that exists, but is not possessed by me, and I desire to possess this thing. The thing might be a car, a boat, a beautiful home, a pet, or anything which, when possessed, is calculated to bestow "happiness" on its owner. It may be a so-called bodily good or it may be a good for the spirit. A hungry man stares into a restaurant window and desires the tempting food he sees; a person to whom art speaks its deep language sees a beautiful statue and desires to own it. The former desired a good for his body, the latter wanted something for his soul to feast on, but each desired in the strict sense.

Desire can also refer to something which exists only in thought and which I desire to exist also in reality. That a certain person should love me can be desired. That war should cease, that I should gain the friendship of a given person, that I should take a trip to

Europe, that I should be promoted in my job—all these things exist in my thought now and I wish them to exist in reality at a later time.[1]

When each of these desires "comes true"—that is, when I at last possess the car or statue or meal, or when at last I take a trip to Europe, or gain the love of a certain person, or am told that war has ceased—the object or event in question has just so much happiness to bestow on me as is in its nature to have. To possess a beautiful statue, therefore, can be the source of much positive happiness but it cannot yield as much happiness, as, say, to have a love requited at last. Again, that a desired truce has come about cannot yield as much happiness to me as that a desired just peace has been established, and so on. The important thing is that the *rank* of the object determines the depth of the happiness that is motivated when there is simply a question of having the object or event existing and present to me, whether it was desired beforehand or not. If, then, a specific happiness arises from the subjective motive of having a desire come true, this happiness will be other than, and in addition to, that which is motivated by the rank of the thing.

This joy, based on the active subjectivity of fulfilled desire, has been called a "subject-motivated joy." It can have at least three different relationships with the object of desire. The latter may be, first of all, a good that really is able to motivate joy; or second, it may be an illusory good; or third, it may be a partially illusory good.

If the desired good's intrinsic contents are able to motivate joy, however slight and superficial, then the subject-motivated joy over the realization of the desire for the object may be called authentic or genuine. In this case, the subject-motivated joy is a real addition to the object-motivated, a bonus which multiplies the happiness that is bestowed by the contents of the good. A precious good, if it is presented to a man who has never even known of it, much less desired it, can give him only object-motivated joy. But if he has for long beheld its splendor from afar, if he has longed for it ardently, cherished it in his memory and hopes, then a great glow of added joy is his when the precious good moves toward him and, finally,

1. See von Hildebrand, *Ethics*, chapter 2.

comes within his reach. The objective contents of the good are the same for this man and for the one who had no desires. But the subject-motivated joy of the "now at last" belongs only to the man of desire.

We may compare the motive for object-motivated joy to a gift which is given without ceremony to a child. Opening a drab package, the child discovers a delightful toy and is pleased because he possesses the toy. The motive for subject-motivated joy, on the contrary, is comparable to a beautiful transparent box that contains the same toy as above but is placed on a high shelf and is viewed and desired by the child for a long time. When the box, brightly decorated with a ribbon and bells, is taken from the shelf and brought to the child, the child experiences the subject-motivated joy of the "now" of fulfilled desire.

We must stress that authentic subject-motivated joy is possible with lowly object- motivated joys as well as with high and important joys. So long as a man desires something which is able to motivate some degree of joy, he can experience subject-motivated joy when his desire is fulfilled. If he has grasped the object in its true rank, estimating it neither too high nor too low, his subject-motivated joy is authentic. In this case it exactly parallels the rank of the object. The rank of the joy, provided always it is authentic, parallels the rank of the object-motivated joy it accompanies. Whether high or low, however, the subject-motivated joy always adds to the joy which the object, considered merely as a "content," is able to motivate.

Suppose now that a given object provides no motive for object-motivated joy, that it is simply a neutral fact which contains no reason for joy or enthusiasm or any other positive affection. We must now ask two questions. First, is an object-motivated joy possible with respect to this neutral object? The answer is clearly negative, for what we mean here by a neutral object is precisely something which excludes all motives for such a joy. Our second question, then, is this: Is a subject-motivated joy possible? We must answer in the affirmative. It is here that we meet the second kind of relationship that is possible between subject-and object-motivated joy—the relationship, namely, between a subject-motivated joy and an *illusory* motive for object-motivated joy. Because this subject-motivated joy is based on no genuine object- motivated joy, it cannot be called authentic; it is best described by the same adjective as describes its partner: illusory.

A deep psychological truth about the nature of certain desires will become clear if we focus on this illusory joy. Using our previous analogy, we may compare its motive to an *empty* but beautifully decorated transparent box. Seeing the attractive colors of the ribbons and the large dimensions of the box itself, we persuade ourselves that we desire the box, contents and all. The fact is that we never bother to look closely at the contents—to see whether they indeed exist and are able to motivate object-motivated joy. Instead, we just assume that they exist and are desirable. We soon find ourselves desiring the box. In the moment when the desire is fulfilled, we experience the subject-motivated joy of the "now at last." This quickly dies, however, for it is a thin joy indeed, not backed up by objective content. If we leave our analogy and speak literally, we may summarize the illusory joy as follows.

When a certain desired object is not yet present, we wrongly think it will give us object-motivated joy. When it is present, when the desire is at last fulfilled, we are moved to subject-motivated joy simply because a desire has been fulfilled. The object itself has no ability to please us, but its occurence or presence triggers the joy we *expected* it to give when it was absent.

One of the best examples of this illusory joy is the spectator of a sports match who rejoices because his team wins. Granted that other motives may also operate (such as his pride in the team or winning money), the chief reason for the spectator's enthusiasm is his illusory linking of what is a neutral event(his team's victory) with his own good fortune. When the event occurs, the fact of a "desire fulfilled"is the ground of his gladness. To be more accurate, the joy occurs because a desire is grasped as *now* being fulfilled, but the desire arose because of an illusory link between a team's victory and the fan's happiness.

This illusory subject-motivated joy may be found in certain other areas of human life besides competitive sports. Whenever, in fact, there is doubt as to the outcome of anything (whether an unimportant election, or a race between two animals, or anything else of the sort), we may arbitrarily choose a special outcome and then desire it. We play a game with ourselves. When the outcome we have favored happens to be realized, we experience a mild sort of subject-motivated joy, simply because an artificially induced desire has been fulfilled.

A third situation must now be analyzed to show how a person's attitude toward something can be the reason for joy that is not otherwise motivated, that is, its real reason is not in the content of the object. We have called this source of subject- motivated joy the reason of "partial illusion." We think of the future possession of an object and we attribute more happiness to its possession than the object can possibly yield once we possess it. To the extent, then, that we establish a link between the object and our *great* happiness, we are subject to illusion and are in no way different from the second case. But because the object *does* have some capacity to bestow gladness, our illusion is not complete. It errs with respect to the depth, quality, and intensity of the happiness, but it is correct insofar as the thing, when possessed, will be the source of a positive consciousness and not a misery or neutral consciousness.

Schopenhauer dwelled on this partial illusion. He called it the fallacy of the "object without the subject," and his analysis of its motive is accurate and profound. Let us see how this partial illusion operates.

I happen to be in a neutral state of mind, neither miserable nor positively happy. I am now made to think about something that does not exist and I find myself desiring that it should exist, for example, a trip to Europe. The travel posters lure me with pictures of Venice and Paris and Rome. Friends who have been there give glamorous descriptions of the cities' splendor and beauty and I feel I can wait no longer. The proposed trip glitters with a quality that I term "good." So far, all of this is normal and valid, but deception enters when I dwell on the trip to the exclusion of all else. I begin to say: "If only I might go on that trip, I should be content and satisfied, and happy." And so it seems. For the desire occupies my attention to the exclusion of every thing else. Because I have allowed myself to exist in a simple closed system, as it were, I easily persuade myself that for me to be happy, only one thing need happen, namely, the trip to Europe.

When, however, I at last go to Europe, I find that although the trip indeed yields all the happiness it has the capacity to yield, I am not the happy man I thought I should be. The reason is simple. In my anticipation and yearning I was pure knowing subject. As subject, as observer of things not myself, I forgot my real self, full of unexplored and now quiet emptiness but ready at any moment to yearn for any of the infinitely varied goods that may be present to it. Putting all these aside, I had stared at the thought of one concrete good. Because it had some goodness, because this part of the experience was not illusory, I had felt a sense of suspended joy; my spirit quickened with delight and held this delight in readiness until I should at last own the object. Then this delicious delight, I was sure, would overwhelm me in its reality, even as it had promised in its suspended, anticipated being. Thus the object dominated the experience. The subject, I myself, was pure knowing person, pure anticipating person. The object which I desired had interest for only a part of me. When, however, the real total ego, which is myself, came to enjoy the fulfilled desire, a thousand new desires came out of hiding because of the thousand new objects that tempted me.

Whoever dwells in desire on a single partial good, to the exclusion of all else, risks being disappointed—nay, *disillusioned*—when the desire is at last fulfilled. Not only does he find himself with new desires which, as we have said, swarm around him once his old desire is fulfilled, but even the single desire which is fulfilled is not so perfect in fact as it was in desire. Having a headache in Venice, being footsore in Paris, having trouble with changing money in Rome—these vexations mar even the fulfilled desire of a trip to Europe.

The state of desire is abstractive. It looks only at the good in question and at all the joys this good will bring when it is possessed. But the state of enjoyment of the good, of realized desire, is never abstractive. The subject, with all his aches and troubles, is the one who must enjoy the realized good. Often enough, the subject is plagued with so many minor annoyances, which never figure in the abstract object of desire, that he fails to enjoy the good as much as he had anticipated.

There are cases, admittedly, where the reverse is true: the realized desire is much better than what we expected. This happens because our original estimation failed to do justice to the object as it really is. We desire something which we erroneously undervalue. When the desire is fulfilled, the higher value of the object makes us exclaim: "I never dreamed it would be this good!" However, this does not prejudice our original thesis that we are victims of a partial illusion whenever an object, *rightly understood*, is entertained in a desire which takes no account of the *full* subject—with all his other, hidden desires and all his aches and troubles.

Let us summarize the steps of partial illusion. An object that is not yet possessed or existent comes before our mind. As we imagine it, our attention focuses on it, to the exclusion of all ills and lacks, whether present or possible. We imagine all the happy moments that the possession or existence of this object would involve. When the desire is fulfilled, in that instant all the daydreams and anticipated pleasures are compressed, so to speak, into the single action of our taking possession. This thrill of the "now at last realized" is far more intense than the joy the object can truly motivate with its objective content. And because the thrill *is* subject-motivated—because it depends on a partial illusion in the person—it quickly dies, or (as the saying goes) its edge is very soon dulled. We can then settle back and enjoy the object in the modest way that its true content allows.

Knowledge

So far we have considered two kinds of active subjectivity which can motivate happiness: achievement and fulfilled desire. Both depend on time; both are dynamic and involve "completion" of something that has begun. A third motive is knowledge as such, which is static in the sense we mean to take it. A joy arises, not because *I* have finally discovered something, after long hours of research, nor because a deep desire for truth (about, say, outer space) has at last been fulfilled, but because *I know something true* right now.

Knowledge of the truth as a subject-motivated reason for joy implies that all our interest is on the *knowing as such* and not on the *object known*.[2] When our interest is on the latter, we may experience object-motivated joy, for we rejoice over certain good things. As we have seen in our distinction between caused and motivated positive consciousness, the entire higher part of man's experiences depends on his contacting certain objects through knowledge. All loves, joys, hopes, convictions, and enthusiasms depend on a prior knowledge of objective contents. When, therefore, we rejoice in the presence of a beloved friend or over good news, our joy is motivated by the object, not by active subjectivity. Knowledge as such is not, in this case, responsible for our joy; rather, the knowledge is simply the indispensable way in which the objective contents are brought before our consciousness. We are as unconcerned with the subjective aspect of knowing in these cases as we are with the projection apparatus when we watch a motion picture. What exclusively motivates us is *what we see,* not the means whereby we see it.

What we want to consider now, however, is the joy that knowing as an active subjectivity can motivate. Is it possible that a man rejoices simply because he knows something, anything? May joy be motivated by something besides good news? The answer is clearly affirmative. Most of us remember having experienced a thrilling joy after we learned some truth—perhaps a formula in calculus dealing with problems of motion. The truth that is represented in this formula is fully different from the good news, say, that we have won a large sum of money. In the latter case (as in all our knowledge of good news), the attractive contents of the object are the dominant factors. The happiness is object-motivated. Knowledge, as such, of the truth is not even considered. But when we learn something in mathematics and rejoice in this knowledge, it is the knowledge-itself-of-the-truth which rejoices us. For where is the good news

2. See von Hildebrand, *What Is Philosophy?* ("Knowledge and Object Thematicity") (Chicago, Franciscan Herald Press, 1973).

in an algebraic theorem? Here, then, is something strange: we rejoice simply in knowing a truth, even though what we know is not especially valuable or precious or gladdening. Perhaps this joy will be interpreted as motivated by the "sense of power" that all knowledge is supposed to provide. But the sense of power, when it operates, deals with our power over natural events. Knowing a law of mechanics enables us to control a moving body and force it to do work for us. But are we not also delighted when we know certain things that have no apparent use? With what natural event is the Pythagorean theorem linked? That it has useful applications is granted, but is it not possible that we know the proof of this theorem and rejoice simply in the knowledge? or must we remain dull and unmoved until we are convinced that this theorem will help augment the food supply or calculate the length of roof rafters?

However profound the joy that comes with the sense of power over nature, however much this sense of power is the real motive for much work and research, it can never account for the delight that spreads over a man's face when he learns or discovers a truth that has no known or immediate link with power. This is especially clear when the man is not at all interested in the use of his discoveries but only in their truth, as happens with many logicians of both the ancient andthe modern school, as well as amateur mathematicians who solve mathematical problems as a hobby and send teasers to their friends as a challenge and amusement. Only a deeply resentful utilitarian prejudice can blind us to the fact that knowledge of the truth can motivate a joy in us for the sole reason that *we know a truth*.

But how is this joy to be explained? We are at first strained and serious;then we get to know a truth and a smile spreads across our face. What we know may not be especially important, but we are rejoiced by the knowledge. This, obviously, indicates the delight the *intellect takes in itself*. The power of knowing lies hidden in us, like a sleeping giant. When this power is actualized, it is as if the giant awakes, flexes his muscles, and goes to work. The joy of *being active* accompanies the knowing. Aristotle's theory of pleasure as concomitant to proper activity is perfectly applicable here. Just as we might say that a real giant was "made for work," we can truly say that the mind was "made to know things and the truth about things." When, therefore, we know anything, we are able to experience this subject-motivated joy which naturally accompanies the "flexing" or activating of our intellectual power.

This power cannot operate in a vacuum, however. All knowledge, no matter how enclosed it is in subjective considerations, always includes a reference to an object. The joy, therefore, that comes from flexing or activating the intellect is not the only joy involved. There is, in fact, another kind of joy, which is very closely linked to this flexing joy but differs from it. We refer to a joy which is *object*-motivated but is concerned less with the specific "material" contents of the object, than with its general "formal" aspects. A brief analysis of this formal object-motivated joy will clarify the exact nature of the subject-motivated flexing joy, the joy of "proper activity."

To begin, we must distinguish knowledge of concrete singular existents from knowledge of "types" or "general" beings." When we become acquainted with a new section of the globe—Alaska, for instance—we learn about many concrete singulars. We see forests for miles and miles, frozen lakes, herds of caribou, beautiful mountains, and so on. On the other hand, when we learn that gravity causes a freely falling body to accelerate, we learn something about a *type*, not a concrete existent. All *experience* is of concrete existents but all *science* is of types.

As we have seen, a given concrete existent is able to yield a material object-motivated joy, provided it has specific contents which glitter in some way, which are somehow attractive. Thus the beauty of parts of Alaska can rejoice us. But let us suppose that what we learn has no specific contents that glitter. Is there any chance that we may rejoice because of a *formal* rather than a material motive in the object?

Suppose, for example, that we explore parts of Antarctica and we see miles of floating ice, often obscured by skies that threaten snow. Granted that certain combinations of ice and sky will be truly beautiful, we can also agree that much will be rather prosaic from the aesthetic point of view. Nevertheless, will not a certain joy be ours as we traverse mile after mile, simply because we realize that we are contacting something real, something ultimately mysterious? We rejoice because we have contacted the "formal" value of being, as opposed to the specific "material" values of beauty or sublimity and the like.

Everything that exists, including the lowliest weed, shines with this formal value of being with more or less splendor, depending on the rank of the being. We are able, consequently, to experience a joy that is mixed with wonder whenever we contact something—anything. This joy is primarily object-motivated, for what excites our wonder is the mysterious *reality* of the object. But just because knowledge by its very nature is destined for reality, we also experience, whenever a reality comes before consciousness and is known, the subject-motivated joy of flexing, Our intellect, it is true, does not greatly flex itself to perceive a singular existent. Still, it is active when it comes face to face with its predestined correlate—the really existing object.

A new and more advanced stage of intellectual activity operates when something general or typical is known. Subject-motivated joy in knowing reaches its climax here because of the high pitch of intellectual activity. The mind really flexes itself. Again, using our former comparison, the mind's activity in grasping concrete singulars and their formal value of being is like the giant's mild exertion in snapping a twig. But when the mind gets to know types, it is like the giant tearing up trees. The joy the intellect takes in itself is at its highest, therefore, when it is activated in its "scientific" use—its knowledge of types.

Corresponding to this flexing joy before types is the joy that is motivated by the formal but objective *logos* or structure of the type that is known. As every singular existent shines with the formal value of being, so, analogously, every typical fact shines with what we might call the "formal beauty of rationality," or, perhaps better, "logical beauty." The inner structure or logic of typical reality shines with a beauty of its own. A new kind of delight and wonder seizes us when we contemplate a type. It shines with "rational interconnectedness"—like a luminous network of underground tunnels discovered by a kind of intellectual X-ray.

Logical beauty primarily "resplends" shines forth from typical reality itself. It is the beauty of objective reason that is grounded in the nature of things. It has, however, what we may call a secondary or reflected existence, which shows itself in a great scientific book about some typical reality. Like a powerful converging mirror, the book captures the objective reasons of the thing and reflects them in its own outpouring of light.

There is, in other words, the objective rationality of the object and also the conceptual rationality of the book that is written about the object. Each shines and each delights by its light. If we first contact the object and succeed in grasping the luminous objective *logos* or structure, we are delighted by the objective rationality of the thing itself. If, instead, we first learn about this object through a book, we shall first be delighted by the clarity and precision of the written reasons; these, if they are true, will lead us to the object and then the objective rationality will come into play. Both the object and the book about it exhibit "reason." Each is a network of accurate, interconnected realities. Each is also a very palpable unity, with all its components intelligibly related. A kind of beauty shines from each and it rejoices us by its structural neatness and precision. Thus we often refer to a scientific or logical or philosophical treatise as "beautiful." We say ". . . as Newton has so beautifully shown" or "as N has so beautifully proved." The beauty in these books is the shining-through of the reasons of knowledge. We have called it logical beauty since it depends on the structure of the reasons and arguments and not on the matter under discussion.

The above-mentioned formal reasons for joy are strictly on the object side and therefore the delight they yield cannot be identified with the subject-motivated joy of knowing. This, as we have seen, is the joy the intellect takes in itself—the joy of flexing. We may summarize, therefore, as follows. Knowledge affords a subject-motivated joy whenever the mind enjoys its own flexing, whether before a concrete existent or a typical reality. Knowledge affords an object-motivated but formal joy whenever the mind contemplates the formal value of being that is found in everything, even the lowliest reality, and above all whenever the mind grasps the objective *logos* of typical reality and sees its logical beauty. The latter appears in a reflected way in scientific books about the typical reality.

As we have mentioned several times previously, Aristotle often identifies the highest happiness with intellectual activity. He never stresses the *object* of this activity, but finds happiness to be a concomitant of the activity itself, considered as an immanent "energizing." After our analysis of the joy that is rooted in the active subjectivity of knowing, it should be clear that this approximates Aristotle's choice for the highest happiness. But how far it is from the truly highest happiness should already be obvious. As we proceed, this happiness, rooted in knowing as such, will be seen to pale more and more when contrasted to the happiness afforded by our contact with high values.

Passive Subjectivity

A new object of motivated positive consciousness is the self as passively related to another person. A different and far more profound form of happiness, a "self-involved happiness," is possible here. As we shall see, the inner core of personal existence, the unique subjectivity of each person, is—in a way—fulfilled and justified only when it is related to another person.

The basic situation which makes all the kinds of self-involved happiness possible, and which even as such yields the same kind of happiness, is *being known* by another person. We can reveal the essential features of this situation by distinguishing it from its chief illusory substitute, namely, being famous. The role of fame in yielding happiness will then be assessed. We will then discuss several affective additions to being known, namely, being admired, being praised, and being loved.

Being Known and Being Famous

If I am famous, it means that I am known by a multitude of nameless spectators who, somehow, have heard about me. Although these persons direct their knowledge and it may be, their acclaim to my total person, my real self, nevertheless they know me only through one or another outstanding deed or work. Sometimes, indeed, the sketchiest rumor of such a deed or work is enough to make me "known" by the multitudes and, therefore, famous. Fame has an "objective," public character. My name, and a weak knowledge of my person, are in the air.

My being known by another person is very different. Whereas in fame I am held up to the public for all to see, in being known by another person it is as if a single spotlight were turned on me by someone who counts. A serious visitor looks at my inner, personal self. My precious subjective existence is acknowleged and accepted. This "being known" yields a classical form of genuine happiness which we have termed *self-involved*. It is not the same as the "banquet" happiness that comes when we dwell amid some great and beloved value. What here takes place is that we are known. Even greater joy comes, of course, when we are not only known but admired, or praised, or, best of all, loved. All these are but deeper and deeper levels of self-involved happiness. Whenever the knowledge or affections of another are directed toward us, whether in our being known or being praised or loved, we glow with a profound and humble joy. How thrilling it is to have our real person known by others, to have visitors to our private subjective existence, visitors who take genuine interest in it and even, perhaps, applaud it in praise or, somehow, respond affectively!

With fame, no such serious confrontation exists. The quality of a secret meeting between persons is replaced by the quantity of many—removed or at a distance from the man. Fame is really a lame substitute for being known. As such, it nevertheless plays an important role as a possible goal to life and work. As we unveil its nature we shall appreciate how important a part it plays in happiness motivation.

Undeniably, the objective fact of fame already secured rejoices many people. Moreover, the desire for a fame not yet possessed is a powerful motor in many careers. How many generals and dictators, how many writers and actors, painters, and industrialists are lured by the desire for fame to do hard things, endure much suffering, or even commit crimes? When we see a man who is gripped by the love of fame, we realize that he is not after bodily pleasures, nor the money that can bring him comfort and ease and pleasure. No, his attitude is completely different. His hand is cupped to his ear as he wonders: "What is Paris saying?" He scans newspapers and listens in on conversations, wondering whether his name occupies a place in the speech and knowledge of others.

Fame must therefore be acknowledged as exhibiting some "goodness," some glittering quality which can motivate desire and, when possessed, joy. This goodness may be of two kinds, direct and indirect. A man who desires fame for its own sake, or who rejoices simply because he is everywhere known, responds to the direct goodness. But if the fame appeals to him simply as a means to something else, only some indirect goodness of fame is at stake. Thus the actress who devours good reports about her proficiency may rejoice for either or both of two reasons. First, the fame itself may please her, flatter her, allow her to see herself shining before the world, which applauds her, gasps at her beauty, envies her successes; or second, the fact that she is famous will ensure a sellout audience for the next six months and thus bring her the money which can procure her what she really wants: comfort, delicious food and drink, a beautiful home, etc.

The fame which is useful, and therefore is sought rather as a means than as an end, plays a great role in the life of many, such as those knights errant who were ridiculed by Cervantes in *Don Quixote*. Such men are cheered by their fame as great warriors, not because this puffs up their estimation of themselves but because they hope to use this fame as an incentive and bargaining point in their effort, so to speak, to win a lady's admiration and love. Because fame of this kind is only a means, we may dismiss it as a motive for joy since it operates only indirectly, to gain other things, different from it, which really rejoice us.

It is therefore to fame which rejoices us for itself alone that we must go to find its place in the happy life. Before we do, however, we should take note of a kind of fame which rejoices us neither because it puffs us up nor because it is a means to an end we ardently desire. It signifies that something really good, something we ourselves have sought to effect, now prospers.

Suppose we have been pioneering a program to persuade people to use vaccines and that hitherto all our efforts received hostile or indifferent responses. Suppose now that the vaccine has at last been accepted and that, as a consequence, our name and work become known to responsible men. We rejoice because we are famous. But our motive for joy is not the image we have of ourselves as standing above the world and receiving its cheers and recognition. Nor is the motive our knowledge that from now on our exhortations will have receptive listeners (this motive, it is true, may also operate). The chief reason for our joy is simply that we see the fame as *confirmation* of the victory of a good thing, in this case vaccination. The fact that people are now talking about us and our vaccine program means that the *program* has gained acceptance. The same joy, but deeper, would be felt by a St. Paul or by any apostle when he learns that the Gospel, which he has ceaselessly preached, has taken root in a nation and has prospered among all the people to such an extent that the apostle's name is on everyone's lips.

We mean now to speak of fame as a motive for joy in the first sense, that is, as rejoicing us by the very fact that we are held up before other men.

A man has conquered all of the known world. He is surfeited with caused, bodily pleasures: the best wines and food, unlimited sex, all comforts and ease. In fact, his bodily comforts are so well taken care of that he is bored. Still, there is something that interests him: the fact that his namme is known all over the world. A wry smile comes to his face when he hears that, even in distant outposts, men speak of him in hushed, fearful tones. He snickers maliciously when a trembling subject implores a favor and reminds him that his name is mighty and that he is known by all to be invincible. Such a man enjoys fame, but fame without praise. In fact, if anything attaches to his fame, it is fear.

Let us observe him a while. Alone, he looks at the map on the wall and imagines all the subject peoples in all the lands. He closes his eyes and hears his name spoken, in stern tones by officers and generals under him, in trembling tones by wretched subjects, in admiring tones by young men who know only that the emperor is mighty and invincible. These visions and sounds rejoice him. He sees the earth as a dimly lit sphere, with billions of unknown, pitiful persons groveling like brutes for a scrap of food, and suddenly his name is flashed across the dark skies for all to read. And his person is mysteriously exalted, so that, shining in fearful brilliance, he hovers before the cowering masses. "I am known and they are unknown", he thinks to himself. "I am someone important, they are nameless dregs—shadows that fear the sunlight of my person,"

Fame of this kind results in glittering eyes, a proud smile, an inner mirth which is cramped and narrow but deep. By a kind of metaphyical irony, however, the joy that comes from this fame depends on the existence of the "nameless dregs", who are so despised, and also on their knowledge that the great man exists. It is similar to the physical height of men. A man rejoices because he is tall and, therefore, not "puny" like many other men. But since height is truly relative, it is only because most men are shorter that the tall man is in any way remarkable.

Fame, in the above sense, gives but egoistic joy, which is partly illusory. On the contrary, the self-involved happiness that comes from being known is a great and authentic joy in human existence. It rests on the truth that our being is not self-enclosed but is open toward other beings, especially other persons. It is not simply that we are "social animals", destined to live in communities in order to survive. No, the "direction" toward others is much deeper, more metaphysical. Our most profound self, our real subjective personal being, is essentially ordered toward personal contact with others. Our unique existence is a secret we long to share with others. We strongly desire to be known, but not necessarily by the world; simply by some few in the world.

This tells us something important. If a man is known by even one other person, if also he is accepted and loved by someone who really reaches his inner being, the man has no *need* of fame. Fame as such, barring its indirect uses, could not cheer such a man in any legitimate way. The gaze of an anonymous public would either leave him indifferent or it would appeal to his pride, or it might even annoy him. But no self-involved happiness would result. If the latter should appear as a result of fame, it would be on the rarely fulfilled condition that the public really knows of some deep value in a man and is *really competent* to judge and appreciate it. Should this ever happen, it is conceivable that fame might motivate an authentic self-involved happiness.

Otherwise, when the public hears but a few rumors of greatness, when also the public is too stupid or coarse to appreciate the greatness in question, a man's fame could have any of four different consequences. First, he might be indifferent, realizing that the many, although perhaps with goodwill, really do not touch his person and do not respond to anything that is genuinely perceived. Such indifference is clearly the right response of a good man. Second, he might be troubled by fame and consider it unwelcome, since it hinders his peace and endangers his humility. Such has been the reaction of saints. Third, he might break into a wry, victorious smile; happiness that is based on pride would fill his consciousness. Or fourth, he might sneer in hatred and contempt for the foolish public which is so wasteful in its praise and attention. The well-known story of the great statesman is pertinent here. When his speech was interrupted by the audience's applause, he looked bewildered and turned to his friend and asked, "Did I say anything stupid?"

We may lay it down as a general truth that all experiences of man that are based on what is right, on what ought to be, are fully authenticated and validated in themselves, whereas experiences which are somehow perverted, which are based on what ought *not* to be, are always linked to an illusion of the subject. Concretely, in this case of happiness we mean this: in all cases of value-motivated or self-involved happiness, the very presence of the value, on the one hand, or the very fact that our real subjective existence is known, on the other, suffices to explain the joy that surges through us. It is completely intelligible and just that we should rejoice in the presence of a beloved; so, too, that we should rejoice because our unique person is known.

When, however, we turn to the happiness which fame normally affords, namely, the ego-centered happiness that comes because our pride is flattered—when, moreover, we observe that many *infamous* deeds are boasted of and are a source of happiness to their possessor—we realize that the positive consciousness that results from such fame is not fully intelligible in itself. It somehow rests on an illusory base. The unfortunates who pursue it are somehow blinded to the real nature of things. But they are not therefore excusable. The whole question of self-blinding is ultimately a moral one and we must always ask *why* an individual chooses to blind himself.[3] Nonetheless, the man who seeks fame is the victim of an illusion. What would really rejoice him, what would send a warm glow of happiness to him, would be his being known even by one, simple person who takes him seriously. Lacking this, he believes that a million blurred faces, none of whom really knows him, none of whom is really competent to judge him, can compensate for the true, clear gaze of even one other person in private.

Is it not continually a cause of wonder that fame should please a man? Even more to be wondered at is that the fame need not be of a man's good qualities. How often we find evil men who grin maliciously when they learn how their crimes and flauntings of justice are known in public. Teenage hoodlums exhibit the same joy that their evil deeds have put their pictures on page 1 in the newspapers. But why should it please a man that he is known as evil, cruel, and malicious? The truth is that what pleases him is not being known as evil but *being known* simply, even if the only way he can become known is through evil.

Indeed we might reflect on this, for it reveals a persistent tendency in our nature: we want to be recognized, to be known, to have our inner dwelling visited by others. A youth hears the remarks of certain people surrounding him, concerning an athlete. The conversation and attention are directed toward this absent person. The athlete is talked about and known whereas the youth is present but unknown, hardly noticed. He may now resolve to *become famous*, perhaps by being an athlete.

But a youth is not restricted to athletics to be famous. Other professions offer similar opportunities. He may study military arts and be a famous general; he may learn medicine and discover a vaccine that will be named after him. In all such cases he shall be known for having done something that is accepted as good by society. But there is still another way: to do something at least foolish

3. See von Hildebrand, *Ethics*, p. 46 ("value blindness").

and even, perhaps, evil. He can climb the Washington Monument and refuse to come down for two weeks, or he can swallow goldfish or submit to some humiliating stunt in public—all this to become known! But he can even do evil things to gain such fame. He can be the neighborhood bully and pride himself on the fame acquired by his brutalities. Youngsters will point toward him from afar and avoid him; their parents will stare coldly at him as they pass by. How elated he is by all this! He is singled out and known. His name is not slurred over and lost; it is articulated, even if only by fearful and disapproving tongues.

Obviously, a normally good man would be ashamed to have his evil deeds known. The classic image of sinners is Adam and Eve, who tried to *hide* from God. So, too, the evils that all of us sometimes do are rightly objects of our shame. We should blush to have them broadcast. But certain men are, first of all, cynical about good and evil and, secondly, so desirous of fame at any cost that they take pains to publish their evil. What they should be ashamed of they brazenly boast of.

All this shameful practice, merely to be known by a nameless crowd! How pitiful are such deceived and self-blinded persons. They do evil in order to be famous. They would be famous in order to be "happy." But the real happiness of *being known* by a single, serious person can never be engendered by the superficial "being known" by a crowd. And so they are victims of *one* illusion. Moreover, if fame is in any way to rejoice them, it must concern their good and admirable qualities, never their evil ones. So these evil men who love notoriety are victims of a second illusion.

We must now note a truth that applies primarily to being known and to the three genuine kinds of self-involved motives for happiness which we mean to discuss, but that applies in a secondary way even to the narrow, ego-centered joy which fame itself may yield. The truth is that all joys that are rooted in self-involved motives depend for their very existence on our awareness that it is our real and not an illusory self which is known, praised, etc. We must feel that we deserve the favorable judgments, the admiration, the praise, the love of another person. Any deformed or illusory knowledge on the part of those who praise or admire us can destroy all the joy we would otherwise feel, for we must grasp that we—and no one else—are the recipient of these affections. If we are mistaken by others for something we are not, their affections are lost on us and can motivate no joy.

This is true even of fame. Despite the fact that fame, in the strict sense, appeals mainly to our pride and our exaggerated feelings of self-importance, it retains enough self-respect, as it were, to insist that it will yield joy only to those for whom it is really meant, and not to pretenders. Suppose, for example, that I am a research chemist in charge of a laboratory, with five assistants under me. One of them discovers an important drug which will benefit mankind. Because of contract agreements or because he is unable or unwilling to take credit for his success, he allows me to publicize the discovery as my own. I become famous. I am depicted as a great humanitarian who works ceaselessly for the good of others without regard for himself. But the truth is, of course, that I was engaged in a different project, totally unconnected with my assistant's venture. Moreover, I am not so dedicated or capable as he and I would never have probed the difficult complexities of biochemistry to discover a life-healing drug. Still, I am famous. My name is known and loved. I am sought after by grateful, admiring, loving people. Can such fame give me happiness?

No. My very knowledge that the fame is not earned, that I stole it is, that if the truth were known I should not be famous, is enough to drive all joy from the fame. I may nevertheless rejoice, of course, because the fame, though not deserved, will be a means to a better salary, a more advanced position, and so on, but my fame itself cannot bring me joy. Even though all fame in some way appeals to a man's egotism, it is, for all that, substantial enough to insist that the man deserve the fame. In other words, even the egotist sees that the joy of fame comes only on condition that he have a qualtiy which is displayed before the world. The man whom fame can rejoice must first of all be happy with himself as a unique person; only then is he cheered when he learns that his hitherto secreted self is now before the eyes of the world.

However, the man who steals the title to fame is conscious of his theft. While he remains thus conscious, he is full of shame before himself—uneasy, too, because he possesses stolen goods. He may also pity or ridicule the crowd for being so generous in its ill-founded applause. If, on the other hand, he suppresses within himself the truth that his fame is unearned, the joy he receives may be compared to the joy that daydreaming affords. One makes believe he is mighty and handsome and basks in the fantasized glory of being known and admired by the multitudes within his dreams. But these are fictitious people, applauding a fictitious individual. So too in real life: the people, though real, applaud something which is fictitious and their applause can bring no joy to the man they applaud. For the people really applaud the *possessor* of the perfections, and the man knows that this is not he.

Unlike fame, being praised, admired, loved, and appreciated are very much at home in the *private* sphere. They are not blurred sounds from vast darkness but clear, forceful, articulated voices that have the effect of cheering the man they reach. One person's praising or loving or admiring me can mean more joy to me than my fame before the whole world. Let us look at these surprising data and see how much our happiness is altered by the attitudes of other persons toward us.

A simple way to begin is to realize that a man is "just himself" at any given time, with all his failures and successes, his good and bad qualities. The man, however, besides *being* himself, also has knowledge of himself. Some of his good qualities, perhaps, stand out in his self-knowledge. His weaknesses may be less prominent than his strengths in this self-portrait; or he may even be proud of his weaknesses and boast of how "human" he is. In any case, the man thinks he knows what sort of being he is.

The self-knowledge a man has, however, is subject to several qualifications, and two distinctions will clarify our meaning. The first is between implicit and explicit self-awareness. Every man who performs anything consciously cannot but realize that he and no one else is responsible for the action. Again, every man who is brilliant in some respect must realize somehow that he possesses this perfection. But in certain men this self-knowledge will always be in the background—it will be only implicit. In other men the deeds and perfections become objects of scrutiny and appreciation. This can easily happen when one person is forced to compare himself with another because the latter has received a promotion or gain because of some supposed perfection. The man who has been passed by then says: "Am I not as good as he? Am I not a reliable, intelligent, energetic?" All rejected men, all who seek in vain for a prize, are forced to compare themselves with the victor. The comparison, if honest, results in what we call "explicit self-knowledge."

Our second distinction concerns only those who have explicit self-knowledge. One type of man will be truly humble about his explicitly known perfections. He will not boast of them, whether to others or to himself. He will not even dwell on them in a kind of knowledge-prelude to self-admiration. He contents himself with knowing that he has certain abilities and perfections, and he tries to use them well. Another type of man, however, will relish his own perfections. He is well pleased with himself and he delights in thinking about his gifts. Such a man lingers before a spiritual mirror, so to speak, and is charmed by the thought that he is a great general, or a complicated painter, or a great success with women—whatever the case may be. To say the least, this man admires himself.[4]

This man is obviously pleased when others admire what he finds admirable in himself. Indeed, he often strains to discover whether others really appreciate him as he himself does, since the joy he derives from admiring his perfections is based on pride. The added joy he experiences when another admires him is equally based on pride. The onlooker merely doubles the pleasure, for now there are two who admire him instead of one. We must admit, however, that an altogether different kind of joy, based on the genuine self-involved motive of being admired, *can* be found alongside the subjectively satisfying joy that is based on pride. But just because this type of man is proud in the first place, it becomes impossible to isolate the self-involved joy and measure its exact contribution. This type of man, therefore, will not suit our purpose.

We may say, moreover, that even admiration that is directed toward one who is humble in his explicit self-knowledge is too dif-

<hr>

4. See von Hildebrand, *Morality and Situation Ethics* (Chicago: Franciscan Herald Press, 1966) for a complete discussion of the pride of self-glory.

ficult to isolate for its effects, for as soon as one becomes explicitly aware of himself he may easily be lured by his own egotism (which never really dies) to be pleased by the remarks of others simply because they flatter him.

If, instead, we consider the man who has merely implicit self-knowledge, we can more easily discern the effects that another's admiration has on him. For such a man does not *expect* admiration. In fact, he is surprised by it and this surprise is interwoven with the joy he feels. Always implicitly aware of his perfections, he finds another person who responds to them and he is cheered by the other's response. We cannot minimize the influence onlookers have vis-a-vis the man's joy. The onlooker has it within his power to cause a profound emotion in the man simply by uttering or otherwise indicating his feelings about the man.

We shall begin by having the onlooker respond with admiration, next he shall respond with praise, and finally with love.

Admiration

A man is a great and daring adventurer. In war, he displayed brilliant powers of survival and attack; in peace, he goes into forsaken places, at great danger to himself, and comes back unharmed and even more self-confident. Though he never explicitly thinks of himself, he has an unspoken, warm regard for himself as adventurer. Moreover, he genuinely enjoys the excitement and the risks of his sallies against wilderness and danger. Suppose now that a second person, a youth, gets to know the adventurer and then to admire him. The youth glows with affection when he thinks of his hero and is flushed with excitement when the admired one comes close. But if the latter know nothing of the youth's admiration, he is untouched by it. Now, however, let him somehow learn that he is admired; let him be told that the youth looks up to him and regards him as a wondrous, dazzling person. Such information is not indifferent: the one who is admired is now able to feel a "wave of warmth" from the youth to himself. A real link now exists with the youth and it is a source of a kind of joy to the adventurer.

How can we explain this joy? The admiration of the youth does not yield a caused pleasure, nor is it useful for anything. It nonetheless pleases the one who is admired. Why? The answer seems to be that the youth is a *witness* to what the adventurer implicitly thinks is some perfection in himself. He thinks: "Here I stand, with many treasures; now at last someone *sees* them, someone stumbles upon certain good things in me, and he is pleased with them and startled because they are so brilliant".

That this is the true explanation is supported by the following consideration. Suppose that I have purchased a robotlike machine which performs many wondrous, almost magical tasks. It can, for example, "listen" to a request for a certain piece of music and play the piece on a guitar that is attached to it. My friend sees and genuinely admires the machine. He gives it the same appreciation that I did. How pleased I am with his response! How happy I am to know that he too *sees* the wonderful quality of the machine and is dazzled by it. But what really stamps this kind of joy in me is the clear realization that the admiration that is tendered to the machine somehow accrues to me because it is *my* possession. If, on the other hand, the two of us admire a machine in a museum, we should have a sympathy with each other because we share similar responses to one object.

But the case we have quoted is different. My joy comes because another admires *something of my own*. The joy, of course, would be proportionately greater if the admired object were a personal attitude or perfection of mind and not merely a possessed thing. In fact, the joy would be of a different quality. A possessed thing is my property. My choosing to own it reflects something of my personal self; thus admiration directed at my property finds its way back to me. But when the admiration is directed in the first place to me, to some part of my personal being, I am gladdened in a deeper, richer way. No doubt, even this joy admits of degrees and further qualitative subdistinctions, depending on what personal feature of mine is admired. That someone admires my bodily strength or agility cannot gladden me in the same way as someone who admires my courage or artistic tastes.

In summary, we may say that admiration is ultimately directed toward certain personal qualities. When they are found in me and admired by another, I rejoice because the other has found some real "possession of mine pleasing." There is something of triumph for me. I am found with something precious and good in my possession.

Praise

Praise that is directed toward us has a more serious quality and depth than another's mere admiration of us. Both, of course, presuppose our being known, which, as we have seen, constitutes grounds for a self-involved happiness. When we are admired it is as if the other finds us dazzling. We, looking at his amazement before us, are rejoiced because our person is deemed admirable. But when we are praised the praise is not merely the other's response, which is now simply part of the other's attitude. No, the praise must be somehow *uttered to us*. Secret admiration is always possible; so too is secret love. In these cases, the other is filled with a response to some quality in us, and this response, whether of admiration or love, now exists as part of his consciousness. If I should learn of it, through information by a third person or through the hard-to-conceal expression on the other's face, I should be rejoiced. But praise depends on a different sequence. It is not a response to a quality one finds in us; it is rather an *activity* of the other which is meant to reach our knowledge. Hence, even to exist, praise must be communicated. Secret praise, therefore, is an impossibility, a contradiction in terms.

It is a well-known fact that praise can rejoice a man. This is so obvious that shrewd men habitually use insincere praise (even totally undeserved) to flatter their partners in dialogue. We are so touched by praise—often so eager to receive it—that the one who utters it soon has the key to our heart. This misuse of praise, however, in no way negates the fact that, in certain cases, praise which is sincerely meant and well deserved can touch us deeply and stir profound joys in us.

Two kinds of things can be praised in us: on the one hand, our *morally relevant* deeds, actions, and áttitudes; on the other hand, our works of the spirit. The latter include scientific and philosophic treatises, poems, novels, sculptures, and the like. Now it is true to say for both things that the praise must be deserved, and known to be deserved, if it is to cheer us. Again, in both cases the one who praises must be competent. He must really know the worth of the things in question.

Let us turn first to works of the spirit. Any of these works—such as a painting, a treatise in natural science or philosophy—can have one of two central themes. Either it is centered around the question of *truth* in a particular branch of study or it is centered around *artistic beauty*, whether in letters, music, or the plastic arts. Now the author of any such work—for example, a painting—can be motivated to accomplish it either by the beauty he seeks to express or by the fame and fortune that a beautiful painting will bring him. Even if the latter is his motive, he still must be concerned with the beauty. For though he treats it as a means, it is still *beauty* (and not something else) that will really bring him fame and fortune.

The same holds for the author of a work that deals with the truth of something. Of course the purest motive, in fact the only one that ensures completeness and seriousness, is the motive of truth itself. The author writes the book, or performs the experiment, because he wants to know or to tell the truth about such and such an object. Here too, however, he can use his treatise as a means to fame and fortune, but here, too, the treatise must be seriously concerned with the truth. For again, though the truth is only a means, it is *truth* (and not something else) that will accomplish his ends.

An author of works of the spirit, then, is constrained by the nature of things to succeed in bringing either beauty or truth into his work. In the event that he succeeds, he will of course know it, for beauty and truth proclaim themselves and are their own best criteria. No man need await the decision of his critics to find out whether his work is true or not, beautiful or not. When a man realizes that his work is beautiful or his treatise is important and true, he receives happiness of several kinds, including the subject-motivated happiness of achievement and the object-motivated happiness of watching a value come into being.

Suppose now that the man's work is praised. Can this bring him new happiness? Obviously it can. The important question, of course, is whether the one who praises is competent. If not, the one who is praised feels only pity and disgust, to hear an incompetent person praise his work. But if the critic who bestows praise is competent, the author is rejoiced. Why? Does he rejoice because his subjective existence is judged a success by another person? Is the praised one found *morally good*? Not at all. Though the treatise in philosophy or chemistry be true and important, though the paintings and sculptures be as beautiful as Michaelangelo's, the author is not, for all that, a *success* in any moral sense. He has not, for all that, fulfilled his task in life and rendered a satisfactory account of his inner personal being. Why, then, should praise rejoice him here?

We must note the following. The man has bestowed time and effort on his work with a view toward perfecting it in truth or beauty, even if he intends that this truth or beauty be but means for fame and money. Now insofar as he is concerned strictly with fame and money, praise of his work rejoices him only because it suggests that his work will prosper and that, consequently, his ardent desire for fame and money will be fulfilled. Also, there is a second consideration: whoever praises the work praises the author. It is possible, therefore, that the author's pride is flattered when one praises his work. He may picture himself as a great genius, rising far above the mediocre spirits in his field. Thus, even though his heart is on success, fame, and the life of ease that money can bring, he may not be averse to drinking in the praise that comes as a by-product of his effort.

On the other hand, the author may be quite serious about the work and indifferent to fame and money. He may expend great labor on the work because he wants it to be true or beautiful. If, in such a case, a competent critic praises the work, the critic can be the source of a double joy to the author. First, the author will rejoice because someone else responds appreciatively to a work which he too loves and enjoys. In this event, the author will interpret the praise as springing from admiration and appreciation. What rejoices him, then, is not so much the praise as what is implied by the praise, namely, a sincere and thorough appreciation of the work itself. This kind of joy is similar to the joy we feel when anyone is sympathetic to our view about a certain value, whether the value has been created by us or by another.

Second, the author will rejoice because the praise of the work means praise of his effort to create a worthy and serious instance of beauty or truth. Even though no *moral* question is in the foreground, even though the effort is not necessarily directed to morally relevant values, the author is committed to the work by all his careful actions and efforts. Like a father doing his best to rear a child, like a master trying to instruct a pupil, the author has labored to create a finished product. When the result is praised, the praise reflects on the author of the work and says"Well done!"

This does not mean that the author's total, innermost personality has been vindicated, for such an ultimate vindication comes only when a competent superior praises the morally relevant deeds and attitudes of the person. It means, however, that a serious part of the author's life, his laboring on behalf of the work, has been acknowledged and found good. The joy that comes from praise of this kind is by no means a subjectively satisfying joy that is based on pride. The author has, if anything, a humble attitude toward himself. He gives all he can to produce a good work. When he is finished, he is rejoiced if someone sincere and competent comes and says: "Your labors have not been in vain. What you have discovered is true [or] What you have wrought is beautiful. Well done!"

We turn now to those cases where someone praises our morally relevant actions or attitudes. For convenience, we shall call these things our *deeds*. To be praised because of our deeds can be a deep source of happiness. We can get a much clearer grasp of this kind of praise if we first elaborate several distinctions about praise in general.

One kind of praise may be characterized as "singing the praises of something to someone." This kind of praise is widespread. Whenever, in fact, we experience a positive and enthusiastic response to some value—perhaps a beloved person, or a beautiful work of art, or a courageous deed by a statesman—we experience two distinct realities. The first is the response itself, an interior emotion which fills our spirit. The second is the strong desire to *exteriorize the response,* "to sing it aloud," to let the whole world know how we feel. Thus understood, singing the praises of something is not praising in the strict sense. The latter, as we have argued, absolutely demands that the praise be spoken to the one who is praised, whereas in the case we are now considering the "praise" need not even concern a person, much less need it be spoken to a person. For we can sing the praises of our beloved lady to a third person without the beloved's knowledge. We can, moreover, sing the praises of springtime, of a beautiful cathedral, of a charming and playful animal, of our country.

Singing the praises of something therefore, has little relation to the happiness of the thing that is praised. If anything, it is the praising one who rejoices. His joy is based on a value response. He is so enthusiastic over the treasure he has discovered that he desires to rally other persons to his viewpoint so that they too might enjoy and admire the precious value. The typical formula for singing the praises of a thing is "Come! Let us pour out our praises upon this value which I have discovered."

A completely different situation is revealed in the case of a boy of 12 who volunteers to receive no Christmas presents from his family because he wishes that the money for them be given to a poor child down the street. His father praises him and says: "You have done well, you are a good boy." Who can deny that such words of praise from someone in authority are a source of deep joy? He will glow with such warmth that he may seek to perform other good deeds, simply to win the praise of his father. Obviously, this attitude would be imperfect from the moral point of view. The fact remains, nevertheless, that being praised for the first, sincerely-meant deed really cheered the boy. Indeed, it had such a delicious quality that it tempted the boy to do good simply in order to win more praise.

This is praise in the strict sense. It is spoken directly to a person by someone who, besides being competent in knowledge, has some kind of authority over the one who is praised. Moreover, what is praised is not a work of the spirit but a deed; more exactly, the boy himself is praised because of his good deed. Praise in this strict sense shall be termed *paternal praise.*

Let us note the chief properties of paternal praise. First of all, it exists only in a direct *I–Thou* confrontation. One person, by words or appropriate gestures, directly praises another person to his face. Second, there must be a difference in rank between the two persons. The praising one must be the superior of the praised one in some moral, authoritative capacity. It is impossible for persons of equal rank, with neither having authority over the other, to engage in an I–Thou situation of paternal praise. Just as impossible—and even grotesque—would be an alleged paternal praise proceeding from someone of low rank to his superior in authority—praise from a boy to his father, for example, because of the father's good deed.

The above statements can be clarified with a few examples. Suppose a man discusses a past deed of his with a friend. The man relates that he had been approached by an ill-clad and obviously alcoholic beggar, asking for money, and that he had refused him money but had offered instead to buy a good meal for the beggar. The man who related this story now asks his friend whether he had acted wisely and, furthermore, whether his deed was morally good or even, perhaps, morally obligatory. The friend discusses with the man the relative wisdom of giving food instead of money to alcoholics; he decides it is wiser to give food, and he may commend the man for his wisdom. Suppose the friend decides further that it is at least morally good, if not obligatory, to help the needy with food. Can we say that the friend thereby *praises* the man for his good deed? The answer is clearly in the negative. The entire discussion between the man and his friend has the character of an intellectual inquiry about a certain being or "typical situation." Both men try to discover truths about the wisdom and morality of a certain kind of deed. Even though one may commend the other for acting wisely, or may even give his opinion that the other acted in a morally good way, neither the commending nor the opinion is given from the "throne of authority." Instead, one man speaks to his equal.

How different the situation would be if the friend attempted to praise the man in the strict sense! This would imply that the friend arrogates to himself a higher level—one with authority. From this figurative throne he would say to his subordinate:"Well done! I praise you for your good deed. You have pleased me by your actions and I mean by this praise to *approve of you.*" In the case of two friends, such a speech would be absurd, for by what right does a man say to his equal: "You have pleased me; well done?" Of course, it may happen that a man voluntarily submits himself to another man and promises him obedience. This submission brings about a real situation of authority, and it then becomes possible for the superior to say "Well done!" When he notes a praiseworthy deed of his "adopted son." But in such a case the men are no longer equals. They ceased being equals from the moment one submitted himself to the authority of the other.

Paternal praise, because it can proceed only from someone who is in authority over us, always has a note of solemnity and gravity. It touches us in our very depths; it approves our innermost person— our self on the moral level. Because of this, paternal praise yields a stirring self-involved joy. In the intimacy of an I–Thou situation, we find that our personality (on the moral level) is dramatically brought into the focus of another's gaze. And the other, looking us over, approves. He says: "Well done!" We thereupon rejoice, for we are acclaimed a success by the only one who really matters, namely, someone in authority over us.

If we compare paternal praise of our deeds with other kinds of praise, we shall appreciate its singular character and its special ability to yield us a deep joy. No other praise can stir us to our depths and bestow upon us the same quality and intensity of self-involved happiness. If, for example, we create an outstanding work of the spirit, we may rejoice if someone who is competent sings its praises, even to our face. But this joy is mild compared to the one given by paternal praise, for a work of our spirit is not nearly so close to our real, innermost person as is a deed. In fact, the work has a distinct, almost autonomous existence. We are its author, we have conceived it, given birth to it and nourished it; but it is now on its own, so to speak. If someone sings its praise, we shall rejoice because the praise reflects from the work and ultimately reaches us. But such praise can never reach our moral core. We cannot experience the joy of having ourselves acclaimed a moral success by one who is in a position of authority, who is concerned with just this kind of success.

Suppose that we have done a good deed and that someone learns of it and sings its praises to other people. This case, so similar to paternal praise since it concerns a deed and not a work, is yet so different that a brief analysis will again prove the singularity of paternal praise. The point to be stressed is the difference between the following. First, A sings the praises of B because of B's good deed, and B learns of it. Second, A praises B to B's face because of the deed. As we have seen, the second case is impossible if A and B are equal. But as we can also see, the first case is possible even if the two are equal. The first case, then, is clearly not the same as paternal praise. A's singing the praises of B may rejoice B when he learns of it. But because A has no authority over B, because A *does not count* in any moral sense, B does not experience the joys that would come from paternal praise.

Besides paternal praise, which is praise in the strict sense, and besides singing the praises of something, there is a third kind of praise, which we shall call "confessing praise." Just the opposite of paternal praise, it goes from a lowly person to a higher one. In fact, we should say that it goes only from a humble, created person to God. This kind of confessing praise is often ascribed (by poetic extension, to be sure) to all the values of nonpersonal created nature. It is, then, likened to dumb, silent praise, a cloud of incense that rises up to God and lauds him, or to a mantle of beauty that is worn by the created universe of impersonal things. The latter cannot speak; so they praise their Creator in the only way they can—by radiating their beauty upward to him. This dumb praise can sometimes be interpreted as "singing the praises of the Creator." This is no doubt the sense of the canticle of Daniel:

> Let the earth bless the Lord,
>   praise and exalt him above all forever.
> Mountains and hills, bless the Lord;
>   everything growing from the earth, bless the Lord;
> You springs, bless the Lord;
>   seas and rivers, bless the Lord;
> You dolphins and all water creatures, bless the Lord;
>   all you birds of the air, bless the Lord;
> All you beasts, wild and tame, bless the Lord;
>   praise and exalt him above all forever.[5]

It is as if a personal creature exhorted the impersonal natures around him to join him in grasping the splendor of God, in responding with love and enthusiasm, and in singing aloud his praises. At

---

5. Daniel 3:57–88. The entire canticle was part of the hour of "Lauds" and now is found in Sunday morning Prayer in the revised Breviary.

other times, however, the "dumb praise" of creation refers to the objective situation mentioned above, wherein the values of impersonal nature testify to the glory of their Creator in a silent but meaningful way.

Apart from poetic extension, however, confessing praise always originates in the consciousness of a personal creature and is directed to the Thou of the Uncreated Person. The one who praises does not think it is his task to approve the Exalted One from a throne of superiority. On the contrary, his praise is humble and lowly and at first whispered, because it is understood to be unworthy, yet gradually it is spoken more loudly and confidently, when he realizes that such praise, such loving acknowledgment of the Other's splendors, is most appropriate and called for, even though the praise is minute and most imperfect. Confessing praise, of course, yields no self-involved happiness to the one who is praised. This truth is obvious, for this praise, unlike paternal praise, does not approve the one who is praised; does not say "Well done," does not, consequently, focus upon the inner subjectivity of the one who is praised and declare from the throne of authority that he has succeeded in his task.

If any joy is involved with confessing praise, it is to be found in the one who praises. He has been smitten with the splendor of the Exalted One, has fallen in love with him. To the former's great joy, he finds himself able to confess his wonder and admiration, his love and enthusiasm for the Exalted One. He finds that he is able not simply to sing his praises aloud but to speak them to the very Person concerned, to "confess" them to the Exalted One. This is the joy of the lowly: to dare to praise the Exalted One in his presence.

Something analogous to confessing praise by a personal creature to God occurs when a lover tells his beloved how precious and beautiful and good she is. In this moment, he also sees himself as vastly inferior to the praised one. Still, it is his joy to praise her to her face—not so as to rejoice her with approval (or worse, with flattery) but to experience the liberating privilege of looking up at something precious and exalted and saying: "Thou! Thou art a jewel, a shining sun; and I know thee, speak to thee. How good this is!"

Being Loved

The last self-involved motive to be discussed in this chapter is "being loved." Unlike being praised with paternal praise but similar to being admired, it is a special *response*, directed toward us. The love exists in the consciousness of the other. It need never be uttered. It can, of course, be expressed by his or her face and body: by the warm, serious look in his eyes, by his visible excitement in our presence. We can learn of the other's love in any of three ways: by perceiving the expression on his face, by his utterance, or through a third person, who informs us of the love.

The key which explains the joy that comes from being loved is this: our joy depends on *who it is* who loves us. In all cases where we love a person and then learn that this person also loves us, our joy is immense, profound, liberating. We are, as it were, ravished with the realization that the precious beloved loves us. This joy of *requited* love will be discussed in the next chapter; for the present, however, we must note that there are many other cases in life where we learn that we are loved by a person who does not even interest us. This often happens in love between the sexes.

Let us think of a young collegian who has wide interests in academic and social affairs. He goes out with several young women, and enjoys their company, but is not in love with any of them. He then learns that one of them loves him. This news does not rejoice him; it might worry or trouble him; it might even annoy him. Especially would news of being loved annoy him if the loving person were a woman he positively disliked or had an aversion to. Of course, the news of being loved by *any* woman can always flatter his pride and evoke in him a smug, subjectively satisfying joy, mixed with pity and contempt for the unfortunate lover. But we assume that pride is quieted, that his conceit is in no way flattered. Shall we say, then, that—at best—only indifference can result from his knowing he is loved, that—at worst—he shall feel troubled and upset over finding himself in a position of being loved by one who cannot interest him?

At first glance, this answer seems inevitable. But if we prescind from the "being troubled" which must come to every man of good will who finds himself loved by one who does not interest him, and if we survey other areas of the man's consciousness, we shall find that a certain joy is motivated in him even in this case. It is no small thing for a person to love another. Always assuming, of course, that the love is serious, and not flighty or neurotic, we grasp that the lover undergoes a deep experience. Whoever she be, whoever it be whom she loves, if only she really loves, she reveals a certain grandeur and stature now that she loves. Her loving another ennobles her, actualizes some good part of her. Nothing small happened when she fell in love; on the contrary, an entire person, a world of consciousness, was invaded by the beauty of another and was transformed into a *loving* person.

If it is no small thing to love, likewise it is no small thing to be loved. However little she appeals to her beloved, however much he is troubled *for her*, because he realizes he can never requite the love, he is touched and rejoiced by the warmth which love always sends to the beloved, even the reluctant beloved. She loves him— this means she has discovered in him something lovable! It means she has singled him out from the blur of other men, has focused her gaze on him and now loves what she grasps in him. She radiates a warmth; she turns toward him a friendly and intense and awakened and imploring gaze. There is a gesture of softness and helplessness in her love.

The beloved's realizing all this has a twofold reaction. First, she appears to grow in his sight, to be more serious, to be taken more seriously—because she loves. And then, because she is taken seriously and thus is no longer an insignificant nobody but a full world of consciousness, ennobled by her loving, he is mildly and cautiously rejoiced by the fact that she loves him. Of course, he would infinitely prefer that he be loved by those whom he loves; nevertheless, he reflects, it is a great thing to be loved. For only another person can love him, and when another *does* love him, it means that his subjective existence, his real self, has entered the orbit of another subjectivity, has been welcomed by the latter, has even "succeeded."

There is, then, this mild happiness in being a reluctant, unrequiting beloved. In the midst of multitudes the loving one suddenly stands out and shines as, simultaneously, the crowds become grayed and blurred. Suddenly the beloved feels fixed on him a loving glance—alone, friendly, and interested in him, apart from the thousands of indifferent hearts and glances that surround him.

How similar to proud joy and yet how far removed is this rejoicing of a man because he is loved. If a man learns that a woman is in love with him, he can of course easily smile inwardly with proud self-appraisal and say: "Alas! How irresistible I am to this woman—to all women!" He can derive great satisfaction from hearing the sighs of those who compete in loving him. But, given this situation, it is also possible that he may respond with no trace of pride. In fact, his first response may well be sadness that he should be involved in the unhappiness of another person. But if he considers the fact that another loves him, and that her face directs warm and loving glances toward him, he can be rejoiced because he is loved, because love exists in another heart and is meant for him. This joy is in no way rooted in pride.

As there are many kinds of love, there are as many kinds of being loved. We may mention spousal love, love of neighbor, love of friendship, parental love, and filial love. In the consideration of any of these loves we must notice the following. If L, the lover, loves B, the beloved, with a given kind of love, say spousal love, the joy L feels *in loving* is completely different in kind and intensity from whatever joy B feels in *being loved*. Only one kind of love, in any one case, stretches out from L to B. Yet L, in loving, might be on fire with bliss, whereas B is but mildly rejoiced in being loved. Our topic here is the joy that comes from being loved, and we have added the all important qualification: even by those whom we do not love and who do not interest us. We are thus concerned with the different joy B receives when he is loved, now with a spousal, now with a parental love, and so on. As we have seen, the minimum result of being loved in any way is a mild joy because of the warmth directed toward us by so serious a being as a loving person.

We must go further, however. We must bring to light and examine a second and far more important consequence of being loved, namely, that the fact of being loved holds up and reaffirms the value of our own, personal existence. To understand this, we must first of all distinguish those cases where a requital of love is always possible, and is even demanded by the situation, from other cases where the ability to requite a proffered love is a rare gift which is not given to each man in every case of his being loved. An example of this latter class is a man's being loved with spousal love by someone whom he does not and cannot love. To the former class belong all loves between a parent and a child and, also, all relations of amiability between neighbors of good will. It is right and natural and normal and to be expected that a parent love the helpless being who is entrusted to him or her by God. It is likewise right and normal that a child requite this love with a grateful filial love. Any departure from the norm (on either side) would mean an objective disharmony, something that should not be. Again, a man who moves into a new society and is greeted amiably by the group ought to requite this mild love with his own amiability. Such a requital is easy and natural—and it ought to be. If, however, he sneers and scorns at the proffered amiability, he departs from the norm and is partner to an objective disharmony.

The same cannot be said of one who fails to requite either spousal love or the love of friendship in the strict sense. In both cases the situation, as such, does not necessitate an almost automatic requital. Though a man is morally good and normal, and though the person who loves him is a beautiful and good woman, he is not, for all that, obliged by the situation to requite her love. It may be that he finds it impossible to do so, though he have all the good will in the world, for spousal love is between very special people; it cannot flower between just any two persons. Therefore, if either the child or the parent fails to requite the other's love, one, or both, must be blamed; if a man fails to requite spousal love, no blame need be attached to anyone.[6] Again, if another man is amiable to me, I am blameworthy if I scorn and sneer and fail to respond with similar

6. See *Don Quixote*, part I, book II, iv. The goatherd's story about the beautiful Marcella includes Marcella's profound remarks about her inability to requite the loves directed toward her.

amiability—with "friendliness" in the loose sense, the kind we mean when we speak of "friendly natives." If, however, a man desires to have me for a friend in the strict sense, if he desires and offers to share my "favorite room" with me and occupy a close, intimate place in my thoughts and heart, I am by not blameworthy if I find it impossible to requite his love or friendship with a like love of my own. For friendship too, like spousal love, involves very special persons and cannot grow between just any two men, however good willed they are.

We can now make the following observations. To be loved with a "special"love which we find impossible to requite, such as spousal love or strict friendship, gives us only the mild joy of every case of being-loved as such (which we have discussed). It simultaneously evokes concern and sadness on our part, a sense of regret that we can do nothing to help the unrequited lover. No other emotion need be evoked by such special loves that are directed toward us. Again, to be loved with a "nonspecial" or "natural" love (parental, filial, or friendliness), which we do requite, is of course a source of joy for us—greater or less, depending on the kind of love proffered.

But we are concerned with still another question: What joy comes from being loved with a natural love that we do *not* requite? Does a child, for example, feel happiness in being loved by a parent whom the child does not love? Or does a parent receive any joy in the knowledge that his unloved child loves him? Is the scowling, sneering newcomer rejoiced by the friendliness of people whom he detests?

In all such situations, something abnormal exists and someone is objectively at fault. This fact holds the key to understanding such cases. Let us suppose a concrete instance—a mother is indifferent to her child. She of course ought to love the child; it is even reasonable and easy for her to love him. Yet, for some subjective fault in her, she does not. Let us suppose, however, that the child loves her dearly. It is understandable that this love should not even be noticed by the mother at first, for the same fault that prevents her from loving would blind her to her being loved. Perhaps she is part of an adulterous love affair and cares only for "the man in her life" and nothing for her child. In such a case the child is a "nuisance," who stands in the way of her "freedom" and "happiness." Still, the child loves her.

At some later time, when her restless, nervous pace is slowed, she may grasp that the child loves her, that he directs his warm, glowing looks toward her and that his heart is tender and open toward her. In this moment does she not experience a profound joy? She should have loved and she did not; instead, she delivered herself to evil. Then she finds herself loved. She now experiences a restoration of her dignity. She is loved! Someone sincerely loves her—sends a warm, sparkling glance her way. To know that she is loved means that she rediscovers herself, profoundly. If no one loved her, as would be all too easy and natural, she might cling to evil ways in the belief that she is not worth saving. But if even one person loves her, this is proof that some excellence remains in her being, for love cannot be engendered by worthless or evil things. The lover must really find and not invent—lovable values in the beloved.

So even the worst person, submerged in evil but convinced that he is genuinely loved, can find in this being loved a proof of his inner preciousness. A great joy must accompany such a restoration of belief in self. The person, bruised and bleeding (and perhaps foul smelling), stiff and bedraggled from having remained so long in mud, suddenly finds himself mirrored in the love another tenders him. But what is loved, what appears in the mirror, is an upright dignified, clean, and beautiful person. Seeing the identity of that image with himself, he can make the agonizing efforts that are needed to walk upright again. All the while he tries to straighten up and clean himself off, he is filled with delight at his rebirth, at his restoration to human dignity.

In view of the above, we may set down as the principal fruit of being loved this affirmation by another of the preciousness of our selves. Being loved can yield us a mild joy in all cases, even when we do *not need* the love to convince us of our dignity. And when we *do* need the love, when our evil ways soil our dignity and hide the jewel of our preciousness, the love yields us the joy of restoration.

That being loved is also a source of *security* cannot well be denied. But the sense of security is not necessarily a positive joy; it often involves the mere negative happiness of removing our anxiety and worries. Moreover, to feel secure because we are loved means that we somehow requite the love, so that a bilateral bond exists between us and the lover. The real security, in fact, rests on close cooperation between the two. Thus the most secure persons are those who are related in a mutual spousal love. Each is aware of the solid link the other means to forge. This experience of two-in-love, of a powerful alliance against all others, is security in the real and full sense. It is exhibited in Romeo's words:

> Look thou but sweet and I
> am proof against their enmity.

We gladly admit, however, that in all cases of requited love, of whatever kind, security is one of the many fruits of being loved; that, at its highest, it even involves a positive experience of strength and solidarity. Our point, however, is that the principal fruit of being loved, as such—even when no requital exists or is possible—is the joy of having one's intrinsic worthiness and preciousness affirmed by the lover. It is this affirmation which mildly rejoices the good man and has the power to resurrect the evil man, so that the latter experiences all the deep joys of a new birth.

Before we close this chapter, we should note the following very important fact. A normal life in civilized society makes it very probable that every person shall be loved by at least one other person—one of his parents, or a friend, a teacher, or above all a lover of the opposite sex. But if all such relationships fail, the unloved must find it difficult, even impossible, to believe in his worth. Now let such an unloved person learn that he is loved by God, that the most sublime Person in the universe, the One who needs no love, who craves no flattery or favors, nonetheless takes a profound, loving interest in him. If only the unloved believes this, a great happiness will be his, for now he has his worth affirmed by the most perfect authority, as it were. Those who also are loved by other humans must experience a new kind of joy when they learn they are loved by God, even though they do not love him. For, as we have insisted throughout these last pages, to be loved as such, by those we do not love, is something great. We now see why this is so. Our worth is reaffirmed each time someone loves us. Our real self, our inner, precious subjectivity, is affirmed by another in such a way that we experience, not the ego-centered joy of being flattered, but the self-involved happiness of being known and loved—of being found *good*.

Our being loved by God, we must add, has two different stages and results in two different kinds of positive consciousness. God may be said to love first our "ontological" preciousness.[7] Because, as persons, we are such exalted beings, because we have so noble a nature, we are lovable in God's sight. Our knowledge that God loves this ontological good in us gives us the profound, positive feeling of being sheltered, of counting for something, of not being abandoned on a strange planet. If we should ever doubt God's love, or if we should be ignorant of it, our life might impress us as an empty gesture, a purposeless wandering, and we might seem to be uncared for, unnoticed—in a word, abandoned. God's everpresent love, however—provided always that we are somehow convinced of it—has the power to resurrect us from every lonely state and to reaffirm for us, in the most basic way, our worth.

God may also love us because of a second, different good, namely, the "qualitative" excellence of our unique person which we have achieved through our freedom. Whereas the ontological perfection of a man is found in every man, regardless of individual wickedness, the qualitative perfection is found only in morally good men. The ontological perfection is the basis of God's "anticipatory love"; the qualitative perfection, on the other hand, is the basis for God's "final reckoning" love. This love, thus, has an element of praising approval. A completely new joy would be ours if ever we should hear God express this final love toward us in the words: "Come, blessed of my Father, and enter into eternal joys."

7. See von Hildebrand, *Ethics*, chapter 10.

Chapter 5
Three Climaxes of Happiness

Part 1: Banquet Happiness

Several times we have called attention to "banquet happiness" to distinguish it from subjectivity satisfying happiness of all kinds and from self-involved happiness. We now wish to look at banquet happiness more thoroughly, to ascertain the various objects which, when grasped by an alert and gifted, appreciative mind, afford a spiritual banquet of joy to our consciousness. The indispensable condition for enjoying such a happiness is that the mind be at rest. We must no longer attend to the nagging voices of needs and wants. Urges and drives, rooted in concupiscence; attitudes and desires based on pride—all must recede from the foreground of consciousness. So, too, even our self-involved concerns, our interest in our own subjective existence, our *self-love* in the best sense, even this must fade from consciousness. If values are to rejoice us at a banquet, it is necessary that they alone shine with their inner light and that the lights of subjectivity, whether legitimate or not, be extinguished. For even the highest, the deepest value, like the brightest star, is unappreciated and unnoticed when the sun of self persists in shining.

In banquet happiness the person is at first a pure, knowing consciousness. All the activity and content are on the object side. The various objects which make the banquet now stand before the person. His consciousness is formed by them. Any pure-value response will likewise be due totally the structure and inner word of the value and to nothing subjective, however excellent.

The question we now ask is this: What kinds of things have the ability to motivate delight in us because of their specific, qualitative excellence? What are the motives for banquet happiness?

Time and confusion can be saved if we limit ourselves to those things that motivate *joy*, as opposed to admiration or interest. The agility of a trapeze artist, the skill of an athlete, the brilliant stratagems of a general can all be admired by me. My admiration is a feeling and even a positive feeling. It is not painful to admire. Nevertheless, to respond with admiration is not yet to rejoice; and the admiring heart is not yet, therefore, the happy heart. Again, the complexity of a given situation or story can arouse my interest, but to be absorbed in interest is not yet to be happy. The brow of an interested man is stamped with purpose, intelligence, and receptivity, but not with joy. Our task, then, is to find out which things rejoice us.

One very evident source of joy is beauty in all its manifold sides. Beauty, of course, is found in many natural objects and situations. It is likewise found in certain artificial objects, certain works of art which have beauty precisely as their *raison d'être*. Although we are accustomed to hear that no one really knows what beauty is, or that beauty is entirely subjective, so that it is impossible to discourse upon it, the palpable reality of beauty is in many cases so potent that even philosophers, blinded by their own theories, are made to pause before beauty and drink its delightful nectar. Who can look without emotion at a glorious sunset on evenings when heaped-up clouds glower with a hundred different colors as the sun falls? What theory is strong enough to blind us to the almost unbelievable beauty of a forest in autumn? Let us for the present forget that nature often hides scars and sorrows under this cover of beauty. The question is not whether the existence of beauty is marred by the evil in the world but, rather, whether beauty really exists, no matter what else exists. Beauty does exist indeed. And when we are absorbed solely by the beauty before us, we feel joy welling up from hidden springs within us. We are washed with the sweet waters called forth by beauty.

It would be instructive (though unnecessary for our purpose) to catalogue the various natural beauties that are offered to man. A hint of their variety and magnitude, however, may be gathered from one example. Consider one scene, perhaps a mountain, standing behind low hills. For each of the four seasons the mountain presents a vision of beauty. Its appearance by day is almost completely different from its appearance by night but at both times it shines with beauty. Thus one and the same scene in but one segment of the earth yields at least eight modes or visions of beauty. Let us reflect on how many beautiful spots there are on earth and we shall appreciate the ubiquity of this minister to joy: nature's beauty.

Moreover, when we "step back" and see the earth as the "blue planet," as a sphere among many others, we are brought to a new dimension of beauty and our delight is mixed with awe as we stare into gigantic spaces. Again, as we draw closer to Earth and all its details, the world of beautiful miniatures opens to our gaze: small flowers and stones, butterflies and birds—each a masterpiece of beauty. To see all this and to respond to what we see is to rejoice with deep joy.

Man, that most mysterious inhabitant of earth, has often ignored natural beauty but has often appreciated it, and, even more, has consistently added to it by works of his own. The fine arts all have beauty for their *raison d'être*. Thus has man added his beautiful creations, to stand beside those of the Creator of all things. Since our point is but to insist that beauty in art is a source of deep joy, we have only to cite a few examples to prove the point. We can therefore avoid those controversial questions on art which, though interesting as a part of aesthetic theory, are irrelevant here. If a man doubts that humanly created beauty can bestow joy, let him reflect on the following. There is a plain with a slight rise to it, and trees are clustered here and there. In itself, the plain shows some beauty. Then someone erects a beautiful building on the high part, perhaps a Greek temple in Doric style. Trees are added here, uprooted there. The scene has been transformed from a modestly beautiful area into a sparkling, compact jewel. So it is with all beautiful architecture that is erected on the proper natural site. Nature's background, modest or glorious, is made the setting for something even more beautiful.

Someone may object: True enough, that architecture is often beautiful; true enough, that it enriches the natural beauty around it; but this does not mean it brings joy to those who look upon it. Are the people who live in a beautiful city (e.g. Florence) happier than those who live in a drab town? Does joy flash across the faces of those who live amid beauty, and does joy fail to light the faces of those who live in drab dwellings?

Our answer to this objection shall serve as answer to the general problem that is hinted at in the objection. Despite many high-sounding theories of the joys that the beauty of art and nature is supposed to bring, the fact seems all too true (as the objection discloses) that people are not happier for living in beautiful rather than ugly buildings. It is often shocking to notice how blind the natives of a city are to the beauties around them. It seems that beauty can evoke joy in a tourist, as he scans a beautiful building, but that as soon as he settles down in the city, he, too, may lose his grasp of the beauty and be as bored and unhappy as the natives.

That this dulling of our sense for beauty comes with familiarity is a patent fact; but it does not refute our thesis that beauty brings joy. For here, as in every case of banquet happiness, we suppose that the object in question is really grasped, is really understood, for what it is. Only on this suppostion does it make sense to inquire whether a baseball game, for example, is a deeper source of joy than a beautiful building. Obviously, to compare these two objects as sources of joy, we suppose that the person is really conscious of each object in its turn. Therefore we must phrase the question thus: *Insofar as* a baseball game presents me with whatever good it possesses, how much joy can it motivate in me? *Insofar as* a building presents me with its beauty, how much joy results? In either case it is possible, and with respect to the latter it is almost the rule, that we become so blunted by familiarity that we no longer grasp the object for what it is. We must, therefore, point to this psychological fatigue or dullness as responsible for the failure of a city's beauty to make the citizens happier.

A second reason for beauty's failure to move us to joy is our preoccupation with other things and our inability to grasp things with objective attention. It should be obvious by now that the chances of misery in life are so frequent that most men at most times carry a burden that is almost insupportable. Weighted with these negative motives, they pass beauty by, much as a man with a toothache will not notice the beautiful rug in the dentist's waiting room or the music from the stereo.

Assume, however, that we are neither psychologically dulled by familiarity nor preoccupied to the point of distraction with sorrows and pains; then it is evident that beauty, insofar as it is grasped and to the extent that it is deep and meaningful, is capable of inciting joy so intense that we gasp over its presence, and may even shed tears.

Let the doubter go from our first case, 'architectural beauty, to works of theatre and music, which have the advantage over architecture that attention is less easily distracted in a theatre or concert hall than in the street. In a theatre, moreover, an element of interest is usually woven into the beauty of the drama, so that for two hours or so we are absorbed in the spectacle that unfolds. Let the doubter recall his experiences with dramatic art. Did he never see *Hamlet* or *King Lear* and gasp with joyful emotion at the splendor of the lines, the incredible definition of character, the noble thoughts, the beautiful attitudes? The experience is proof that artistic beauty brings happiness. The same awe and joy, the same glowing enchantment which great drama evokes, is also evoked by beautiful music. Once again, only the experience proves the point. But even one experience *proves* it.

We have moved from architecture to drama and then to music, and we might move further, to sculpture and painting, but our point has been sufficiently proved. Artistic beauty is a source of joy. Caught in its spell, we are, during the time of our captivity, suffused with a sweet joy.

The beauty of nature and art, however serious and profound, is not the only or even the deepest source of banquet happiness. An even greater class of values exists: that of the *moral* values of the universe. We usually are surrounded by moral disvalues, it is true; as we saw in chapter 2, they motivate misery in us. To contemplate the murders, lies, dishonest deals, the unjust and wicked practices of men, is to feed on disvalues that engender misery. Now if these evils at last disappear, or if they had never been, our mind would attain only negative happiness, that is, mere neutrality. But if they are replaced by goods of value, if just men and generous deeds and charitable attitudes fill the area around us, we pass to a fully positive happiness that is a banquet happiness even richer than that provided by the aesthetic values.

Any confrontation with moral goodness, whether we personally witness it or hear about it through spoken or written words, has the power to rejoice us. We read of a family that is troubled by a false accusation against the father. A seemingly invincible case is built against him by a headstrong, self-blinded district attorney, but the lawyer who undertakes the defense proves the innocence of the accused. The fact that justice has not failed is a great reason for us to rejoice. Moreover, the enthusiasm, courage, and generosity of the defense lawyer are additional motives for joy. Again, we read of the heroism of officials who risk their careers and even their reputation rather than betray the trust of those they serve.

Values even more profound—above all those based on supernatural principles—can motivate even deeper joy. The great charity of saints, the genuine, overwhelming love they manifest toward God and then toward all men, provides the most complete banquet. It is as if with each new value that comes into our ken a different-color light shines clearly in the darkness. The universe becomes progressively more precious and more enriched as each value enters and takes its place. Meanwhile, we gaze upon them in awe and reverence. Each glowing good warms and rejoices us. Each new kind of value surprises us by its beauty, depth, and goodness. Justice and honesty, loyalty, reliability, and courage are the first to enter. How rich and magnificent the universe now seems because these goods are part of it! How delightful and rewarding for us to sup at this sublime banquet of values! Then come concord, fidelity, purity. Greater lights now glow; we stand in greater awe and are filled with greater joy. Now humility enters, and at last charity. The banquet table glitters with breathtaking splendor. We are more and more thrilled and rejoiced at what we grasp—more silent, also, and incredulous that such glory should be, and be spread out for us to enjoy.

Banquet happiness can be summed up by the remark that all values, ranging from the very modest all the way to the sublime, have an "inner power" to stir us to joy of a specific kind when they move into our ken. Each value bears its own gladdening message, each its own flavor for the spirit to feast upon. If we examine any case of banquet happiness in detail, we see that the joy which results from our standing before a value is due to the value's *touching* us. Banquet happiness, in other words, is a result of our being affected. Passively, we receive the message of each value and we allow ourselves to be stirred by it. The beauty and goodness on the value side advance toward us, warm us, *wound* us. In the very act of being wounded we find our delight, our passive delight. We melt under the caress of the value.

Within the framework of banquet happiness we can discern a progressive deepening of delight as ever more beautiful and important values come before us and stir us to joy. Four grand classes of values, hierarchically ordered, can parade before our consciousness: vital values, such as strength, suppleness, agility; intellectual values, such as brilliance, depth, acuteness; aesthetic values; and at last moral values. Banquet happiness begins with the lowly vital values, becomes greater and deeper with intellectual and aesthetic values, and has its true climax in the joys it affords the man who feasts on the concrete realization of moral values.

But such a climax to banquet happiness by no means represents a climax to happiness as such. Two additional stages remain before the absolute climax of all happiness can be reached. All told, then, we have three levels of happiness, and each level has its own progress to its own climax. The first level we have already seen, namely, banquet happiness. The second concerns the *active* stage of responding to values with love. The third concerns the case in which we love a person and this person requites our love.

Part 2: Loving

The joy that comes from loving in every way surpasses the joy that comes from being loved. We saw in chapter 4 that we are mildly rejoiced when we become aware that another's heart radiates love for us; furthermore, that our being loved, because it is always a proof of our inner worth, can lift us from despair and allow us to regain the true vision of ourselves as something precious. Being loved always implies this focusing on self. To love, however, is completely different. Our own worth is not the central point. On the contrary, when we love we are always conscious of our unworthiness. The beloved captivates us. We thereupon despair because we become painfully aware of our lowly value as opposed to that of the beloved—an inequality of such measure that we have no hope that we can offer an attractive bargain in exchange for the beloved's love. We likewise grasp our unworthiness even in loving, for we see that we offer impoverished love, sincere though it is, to something that is rich and exalted. Thus the great value which each of us undoubtedly possesses, so far from being central, recedes to the background when we love. It shows itself, when it dares, not only in the rags of unworthiness, next to the gold and ermine of the beloved.

To love someone is to respond *actively* to the value that is grasped in the beloved.[1] Since this value must first be grasped, the very grasping makes it possible for us to be touched by its goodness and to enjoy banquet happiness, the first level or stage of happiness. In that stage, the value caresses us and we rejoice in its presence and nearness. It sends toward us its joy-dispensing rays. But let us assume we love the good that possesses a value, say a beloved woman. Now a new principle stirs within us. Our spirit, wounded delightfully by the caress of the value, collects itself into a flaming unity and goes forward toward the value. In our loving her, this advance of our selves toward the precious one yields a joy whose intensity is well known to every lover. We feel love, our love for the precious one, swelling within us as if we were the shores of some mountain lake in spring when the snows melt. Love is like all things dynamic and intense. Love is like a fire that roars within the cavern of self and at last leaps out in flashing tongues toward the beloved. Love, again, is like the swollen lake which spills its foaming excess to the streams below. Whether we liken it to fire or water, our love

---

1. We do not mean by this that love is an *action* commanded by the will, or even an *act* of will itself. We use the word "actively" to stress that loving is not passive but is an "energizing" of consciousness outward in a meaningful way.

rejoices us by its activity, its creative activity, its leaping flowlike rush through our consciousness, its swirling, smooth lapping on the shores of consciousness.

We must stress that the delight which is the fruit of loving, like the delight of banquet happiness before a perceived value, is nevertheless a secondary good. Never can the delight be the theme or central point. In fact, should we ever attend explicitly to our delight in loving or in feasting, the delight would end, the feast would nourish no more. Only when the value dominates our consciousness, only then are the springs of delight released. When we feast, therefore, we stand in awe before the value and, in a "lateral" way, we feel joy filling our spirit.[2] Again, when we love we gravitate toward the precious beloved and simultaneously, feel the flames of our love pass through us as they seek their object; the waters of our love rush past on their way to the beloved. All the while that the beloved alone preoccupies us, when her dazzling beauty dominates our every thought, we feel the joy of loving as it surprises us from within. We are gladdened in our very depths. We would like to dance or burst into song. Our heart enjoys the second climax of happiness: it has feasted on the beauty of the beloved, and has suffered itself to be wounded by the beauty; it now responds with a creative, soaring love and experiences the more intense joy of loving.

Part 3: Joy of Requital

It is not necessary that our love be directed toward persons only. Nonpersonal values, such as beauty in nature, our country or a friendly state that shelters us, a work of philosophy, perhaps even an animal, can motivate a kind of love in us which is genuine and often deep. Love is deepest and most itself, however, when what we love is a person, human or divine. This becomes obvious when we take up the third and last climax of happiness: requital. If we should love what is not a person, our love is limited by the *inability* of the

---

2. See von Hildebrand, *Ethics* (p. 261), for "lateral awareness."

beloved object even to acknowledge the love, much less requite it. A sense of frustration seizes us when, reluctantly, we admit that, say, a forest in autumn, glowing with radiant charm, though it caress us with its beauty, though we move toward it with love, is deaf and blind to our affection. When, however, it is a person we love, there is at least the chance that our love will be acknowledged by the beloved, and also the chance (thrilling to contemplate) that our love will be requited.

Our third climax of happiness, since it deals with requited love, is limited to loves which have persons for their object. The happiness that nonpersons can afford us ends, therefore, with the second climax. Love which has a person for its object can, of course, be of several kinds, namely, parental, filial, friendship, and neighborly love. We, however, in our search for the true climax of requited love, shall dwell on that love which is called *spousal*, wherein the beloved engages us in a relation more exclusive, more profound, more total than in any other love. On earth, such love is found between persons of opposite sex, and it usually leads to marriage. Very analogous to this love is the love that certain humans experience for the Divine Person. (We shall reserve discussion of this type for the next chapter.)

In all cases of genuine spousal love, the lover has already reached the climaxes of the first and second level, for the beloved has already wounded us with her beauty and we have already felt the creative leaping of our love toward her. What remains is the final climax. We breathlessly await the moment when the beloved shall first learn of our love, perhaps through a third person. Even if she somehow knows, we feel impelled to utter it to her and we tremble at our audacity. We have long delighted in her beauty, have enjoyed the banquet of her beauty's caress; we have long felt our love pouring past us and rushing toward the beloved. Now we confess our love, protest our love—but will the precious one be indifferent to our love? or saddened by it? Or angry with our audacity? or will she also confess her own love? What a delight if this could be! What a joy if the precious one should not merely tolerate our love but requite it—should find us equally precious! She hears us confess our love. We wait. She smiles warmly. We are hopeful. A flashing glance of love appears in her eyes. She looks at us and says it is true: she *does* love us. Our joy is intense. How splendid and delicious is our life, how meaningful and soaring is the song our heart sings!

This joy of requited love is known, but only by those who have been blessed enough to experience it. When we reflect that not everyone loves, and that not everyone who loves has his love requited, we see that the bliss of a requited love is not experienced by all, perhaps not even by a majority of men. Many a philosopher has lived in complete ignorance of such bliss—to the prejudice of his philosophy. Of course, those who fail to experience it may no doubt *perceive* it in others; may even experience it, after a fashion, by imagining the bliss that would be theirs if their beloved requited their love. In general , however, there is no real substitute for the experience of the joys of requited love. In any group, the relatively few persons who know the bliss of requited love form a community of their own, based on their sharing a common secret. Poetry and literature, music about love, many passages in the Bible—all become intelligible and meaningful to these few. The song of the Creator is echoed in their heart, the hidden principle of the universe stirs within them. They alone are not lonely; to them alone, life is neither hostile, nor terrifying, nor boring, nor troublesome. They love and are loved! Heart speaks to heart, delighting together.

That this bliss of requited love is dulled and often killed by time is no fault of love and no argument against the powers of love to bestow bliss. It is,rather, a sad indictment of man's weak nature. Everything that is good and precious is liable to be tainted by complacency and corroded by the acid vapors of pride, which ever again rise up from the depths of a human person. But *as such,* loving and having that love requited can give man a real climax to earthly happiness.

Chapter 6
God and Happiness

Thus far we have considered different ways in which a man can experience positive consciousness while he lives on earth. We have seized upon well-known and easily available data and have forced them to yield insights into the nature of happiness. We have not, however, ventured beyond *human persons* as the motivating objects of joys and delights. Instead, we have stopped at human persons and have found in them all the climaxes of earthly joy thus far considered.

It is time now to go beyond human persons to God. Our phenomenology of happiness would be glaringly incomplete and basically distorted if we failed to examine the joy that the Person of God can motivate in man. We understand by the term *God* what Catholics have always understood: the Reality, fully conscious, fully personal, which eternally exists, which supports all temporal existence; which engages in a moral dialogue with the only personal inhabitant of the earth, man; the Reality, moreover, which interjects itself into time and history, first among the Jews, as God singled out Abraham and Moses to receive his revelations, and then among all people in the person of Jesus Christ, truly God, who became a man and lived on earth.

We can immediately make the following distinctions: some men firmly believe that God, so understood, truly exists, that he is the source and final goal of all creation. Other men believe in no such being as God. Among such men, we must distinguish between those who grasp with their natural reason the existence of a personal God, even though they do not *believe* that he has given a revelation to men, and those who deny that a personal God exists or can be known, whether by faith in a revelation or by reason.

We do not propose to justify the Catholic belief in God or even the conviction (rationally discoverable) that a personal God exists. The latter point is an entire treatise in natural theology and the former involves the question of faith in all its complexity. We do not hesitate to affirm, of course, that we firmly believe in God as revealed in and through Christ, and that we are convinced that (Kant notwithstanding) we can rationally justify the central thesis of natural theology, for example, the existence of a personal God.

What we propose is simply this: to meditate upon the profound joys that come to a man who responds to God as revealed in Christ, and upon the less profound but equally real joys that come to the man who somehow grasps that a personal God, the sum of all perfections, really exists. We want to display the *intelligible link* between certain human experiences, in this case joys, and the special objects which motivate these joys, namely, the Person and perfections of God.

What we propose is truly philosophical, for *religious experience* is just as much a datum as ethical and aesthetic and social experience. If the latter are open to philosophical scrutiny, if we can display certain intelligible links in them between experience and motivating object, so, too, are religious experiences open to philosophical inspection. It is a strange fact that many moderns gleefully applaud the venture of psychoanalysis and psychology into religious experience while, at the same time, they frown upon philosophical exploration of the same religious data, and even dismiss such exploration as "pious theologizing." We are convinced that *all* experience, all phenomena that are given in experience, are possible objects of philosophical analysis.

In Chapter 5 we argued that a man can rejoice because he grasps beauty, and again because he grasps the splendor of the value of justice or charity as realized in this or that concrete man. So too we now argue that if a man grasps the existence of God, of the same

God who was adored and reverenced by the Jews of the Old Testament, the same God made incomparably more accessible and known by the revelations of Christ in the New Testament, such a man, we say, can experience banquet happiness of great depth and intensity. For he feasts on the presence of all values and perfections.

If, however, the reader should not be convinced that such a God exists, the reader must nevertheless acknowledge that the man who believes in God is rejoiced by what his belief presents to him. William James no doubt appreciated this truth; by a strange logic, however, he was led to the unfortunate thesis that, since certain beliefs can yield happiness, a man is justified in holding an unprovable belief simply on the ground that it affords him happiness. James failed to see that the believer must hold his belief *as true* if he is to be rejoiced by it. Of course, it may later happen that he discovers he was wrong, in which case he can no longer believe, and the joy that once came to him can no longer be present. But to say a man may hold belief A to be true, not because he is intellectually convinced it is true but only because A, when held, has the capacity to bestow joy, is to give a formula for make-believe happiness, for self-deception. One invites the man to frame a pleasant myth and justifies his daydreaming by saying: It is enough that his myth make him happy.

We, on the contrary, say that no man is justified in framing any belief or theory except on the basis of evidence that impels intellectual assent. Only when he is truly convinced that certain things are so, only when the fact of reality has satisfied the canons of truth, only then can what he knows rejoice him, if it represents something deep and beautiful. If an "outsider" (the reader, perhaps) does not share the same beliefs as the man in question; if, for example, the reader has not been convinced of the *truth* of the statements that a personal God exists, or that Christ is God, the most he can do is say that he disputes the basis for the other man's happiness. For the other man holds that God exists; the reader holds that no God exists. The reader can then pity the other for living in a fool's paradise, in that what moves him to delight is but a fiction in the reader's eye. Nevertheless, the reader must agree to what has been our point all along, namely, that a genuine, deep joy, a banquet happiness of great intensity, is intelligibly linked to the motivating object, in this case, the fact that God exists. The reader, therefore, can even *understand* that he too would leap with joy in that moment, if ever it should come, when his mind grasps the splendor and perfection of a Person who is endowed with all values, an absolute Person, Lord and Creator of the universe.

We now ask, What kind of happiness comes to a man on earth when he apprehends the existence of a personal God? Let us suppose a man who enjoys all three climaxes of earthly happiness discussed in chapter 5. That is to say, he feasts upon great values and is warmed and nourished by their splendor; moreover, one special good, a beloved person, comes into his sphere and he enjoys the new joy of loving. Finally, this beloved speaks words of requital that move the lover to the third, final climax of joy. That such a man is happy in a deep sense is not to be doubted; especially is this so if somehow he is spared most of the miseries that attend life.

This man, as he warms in the sun of great values, as he holds his beloved close to him, from time to time looks beyond the goods that are present to him and stares into the limitless universe. Perhaps he thinks of the total network of the universe as but a vast solar system. On the small planet called Earth, he is warmed by its beauty, both natural and artistic; he is warmed even more by the great moral values he sees realized at times in men: courage, fidelity, generosity, justice. He is deeply touched and ravishingly caressed by the soft beauty of his beloved; he is stirred by his love for her and delighted by her requital. But as he stares beyond this planet, as he surveys that limitless universe, he experiences a chill, a terror at the emptiness and ruthless efficiency of great masses hurtling through space. He is awed, even frightened, by the silent power that is everywhere present—making green plants grow on the crust of the earth, multiplying animals and humans as if by magic, swallowing billions of lives, as if by another, darker magic; pushing huge bodies through space, through lonely, chilling space.

Suddenly he grasps that a *personal God*, different from the solar universe, supports the universe. Suddenly he apprehends that the metaphysical ground of all he experiences, the core of all temporal being, is God—a person, an awakened being, a conscious, alert being. Suddenly all the pieces fit together: the depths of the values on earth; the beauty of his beloved, the overriding importance of this love; the silent, vast power of the stars and sun. The personal God is the source of all this. The values that so caress the man on earth are but refracted rays of God's splendor. So, suddenly, the ecstasy of loving, the nobility and majesty of moral values, the grandeur of power and force in the physical universe—all are rooted in a single, incomprehensible unity: a personal God.

In this moment the man finds a new banquet happiness within his spirit—an intense, gladdening excitement, a surprised delight, an awe that is almost incredulous. A personal God exists!

True enough, this God is not perceived through the senses. How should he be? If God were a body, then a man might see, touch, hear him. But he is a spirit and therefore is not accessible through the senses. Because of this, it requires effort to focus on God with conscious attention. Whereas we need but open our eyes to see a body, even such an extraordinary and splendid body as the Cathedral of Chartres, we must make an altogether more difficult and *unfamiliar* effort when we would focus on God. We must shut out the bodies of the temporal world, with their bright colors and hard surfaces and their tastes, sounds and odors, bodies which clamor for our attention, bodies which so easily capture our attention because they ask so little of us, since they are intuitively given in their self-presence. We must meditate on spiritual things, such as our knowing, rejoicing, doubting, loving, desiring. We must meditate on our personal being and, above all, on our contingent personal being. Then God's being begins to be differentiated: a personal and necessary Reality—the principle of all that we grasp in experience, the sufficient reason of all things that are not explainable through themselves or through any other contingent reality.

Let a man come at last to this conviction, that a personal God exists; let him daily meditate on this startling fact. It will soon become his favorite meditation. God will soon be appreciated as the most precious value in the universe. For all the perfections and splendors of the values that enchant and delight a man on earth will belong in an incomparably more perfect way to their principle, God (whether formally or eminently, as the Scholastics say).

The banquet which God affords will also contain that metaphysical *sheltering* which is completely absent from all fruition of earthly values, no matter how precious. Here is not a being subject to change and corruption. Here is rather an absolute Person, one who oversees creation and presents an everlasting haven to those on pilgrimage. Our contact with God overcomes our estrangement and loneliness, and our anxiety. For we find ourselves at last in the presence of the eternal Lord, the *self-same*, the mystery at the heart of the universe, the goal of our deepest personal strivings.

We can conclude, then, that this grasping of a personal God goes beyond the climax of banquet happiness discussed in chapter 5. For it is a greater and more delightful banquet when we grasp God, the *sum* of all values, than when we grasp but this and this value. Shall we say that at last we have reached the true climax of banquet happiness? Once we grasp the sum of all values, is there anything higher that awaits us at the banquet table? We must answer with a distinction, or rather with two sets of distinctions. We must ask whether the *implicitly* meaningful term, *sum of all perfections*, holds more and deeper surprises when certain values are *explicitly* discovered in God through further analysis, and, it may be, through a new principle of knowing, namely faith. In other words, the man who knows God simply as the "sum of all values" is limited precisely by the values that fall within his range of experiences. If now he has deeper and different experiences—above all, if faith allows him to grasp new things and to see old things with new sight—then the meaning of God becomes more *explicit* and the man's banquet becomes proportionally enriched. We shall return to this point.

Our second set of distinctions revolves on this: man on earth, moving through time, must always make an effort to recollect himself and to focus on God, whether the dimly grasped personal God of reason or the revealed God of faith. If we were to imagine a kind of existence in which no such effort were needed, if instead God were to be as directly and intuitively present to man as a man's beloved spouse is present to him on earth, the banquet happiness of this imagined existence would be greatly enriched, not on the side of the values involved but on the side of man's ability to grasp and enjoy these values.

We may now develop the first of these distinctions. If a man grasps God as the sum of all values, he has in a real sense reached the climax of banquet happiness. As we have noted, however, these values may be only implicitly known. As more and more meaning and depth are explicated in the person of God, the banquet yields greater and greater delights. It is as if all the values were one inside the other, so that the more a man grasps a surface value, the more is he led to the next deeper value; when this in turn is known better, it suggests a yet deeper one, and so on. But how does one explicate the person of God? Since God is grasped as the principle of all goods discovered in experience, he is more explicitly known the more his creation is known in all its differentiations and depths. Thus there is a progressive line *within* the climax of banquet happiness itself. The banquet afforded by God gets better and better, because more explicitly presented, as a man progresses in his knowledge of values that are given in experience.

But besides this natural progress in explicating God we must see that there is yet another way. If God should ever reveal truths about himself, a man would know more about God, and would consequently be treated to an even more delightful banquet. Now faith offers just this chance to a man—for it enables him to believe in the *revelations* of God as given through Jesus Christ. Thus God speaks about God, and the man of faith listens and then *knows*. The implicit knowledge he had of God becomes suddenly greater, much richer, as new treasures are revealed; above all, as the charity of God is revealed.

We have said that faith allows a man to "grasp new things and see old things in a new way." How is this so? The man of faith sees new things because now he can accept *as true* certain revelations of God to man. There is always deep mystery about God, that aloof principle which the greatest philosophers of antiquity (especially Plato) longed to know more intimately after they had somehow grasped his presence "above" the universe. This mystery suddenly becomes closer when a man has faith. Features of God are differentiated. The man of faith learns that the Divine Substance exists in three distinct Persons. He learns what the Jews of old, inspired by God, wrote about the Father. He meditates on the majesty of God and realizes that Moses fell flat on his face when he approached the *living God*. The man of faith learns what the Evangelists and St. Paul (also divinely inspired) wrote about the Son, Jesus Christ, and about the Holy Ghost, as well as the Father. Christ's own words about himself, the Father, and the Holy Ghost reveal the depth and plenitude of the Holy Trinity. And Christ in his humanity expresses divinity, manifests infinite perfections through the medium of finite flesh. The love Christ has for all men, that "charity of Christ which surpasses all understanding," is displayed at this banquet that is reserved for the man of faith. How delighted he is to sup at this sublimely furnished table! Indeed, faith allows us to grasp new things.

It also allows us to see old things in a different light. Since the time of Christ, *sanctity* has been a genuine phenomenon on earth. Certain men and women have exhibited the most amazing change that experience affords. They have been *transformed* from "earthly citizens," with all the attitudes and deeds implied by this state, into "other Christs." As if possessed by a new principle of life, these men and women, and even children, have "put on Christ," have accomplished actions, and have spoken words, and have experienced loves which human nature alone is not capable of. Each century, often each decade, produces at least one of these other Christs, these *saints*. But men without faith generally pass the saints by. Perhaps the former are for a while amazed at the great charity of the saints, their remarkable courage and strength. But soon the amazement is dulled; the saints are confined to human categories invented by those who lack not only faith but even acute philosophical perception. Saints are then called "enthusiasts," or "neurotics." Their extraordinary virtue is ignored, explained away, or even attacked as "weakness" (by such men as Nietzsche).

Then faith comes, and with it the clear light of truth. Things are seen for what they are. The sanctity of certain men is understood as a mirror of the infinite sanctity of Christ. When the man of faith begins to understand Christ, he takes a second, more accurate look at the long-despised saints. "We fools esteemed their life madness and their end without honor; behold now they are numbered among the children of God, and their lot is among the saints" (Wisdom

5:4–5). Armed with the truth, the man of faith is rejoiced when he realizes that the earth never lacks sanctity, that—some place or other—the brilliant jewels of the supernatural values, crowned by charity, shine forth at a banquet that is spread *on earth*.

We have argued that faith in Christ allows a man to understand the beauty and depth of sanctity as it is found among humans and, thus, to sup at an earthly banquet of supernatural values. Often, however, it is the sanctity of humans which leads a man to faith in Christ. There is always, in fact, a kind of oscillation between understanding the saints through understanding Christ and understanding Christ through the saints. We may begin with a slight appreciation of Christ; this will let us appreciate somewhat the true nature of sanctity. Better acquaintance with sanctity, as found in the saints, will throw more light on Christ. Increased knowledge of Christ will give us a better appreciation of the saints. And so on.

The values which we come to know and appreciate in Christ and the saints are *concrete realities*, singular perfections that exist in singular men. They have another aspect, however, another dimension of being, for every value that concretely exists in a man, whether justice or generosity or charity, is a temporal, finite realization of its respective essence or exemplar.[1] In every case the exemplar is immeasurably richer than the concrete instance, for the exemplar is the pure source, the inexhaustible fountain which lends part of itself, so to speak, to the finite instance. Thus no just man exhausts justice; no just law is so rich as justice. For justice is the pure exemplar in which these finite instances "participate" (to use a favorite term of the Platonists and even the Scholastics). The exemplar of any moral value always has this archetypal relation to instances or realizations of the same value. It is the pure source, whereas the instance merely "partakes" of it or "participates" in it. The exemplar is also the *measure* or *standard* of the instance. Hovering above time, it judges the things of time. Actions and attitudes are just or

---

1. The essence of a perfection is often called the ideal or the idea or the exemplar of the thing. It seems to us that, nowadays, *exemplar* is the happiest choice to indicate the Platonic Idea, since it avoids the essence/existence controversy.

not, more just or less just, depending on how they conform to the absolute standard of the exemplar. The same is true for any other moral value. The instance is judged by the exemplar.

All of the above has a very important application to our topic of banquet happiness, for we are now in a position to distinguish the earthly banquet of finite instances of all values from the altogether new and otherwordly banquet wherein the table is spread, not with singular instances but with the very exemplars themselves, the pure sources that are infinitely richer than the instances.

We can set down the following sequence. A man may enjoy, first, an earthly banquet of natural moral values. Thus he grasps men and actions which are just, courageous, and generous. Second, the man may come to know and rightly appreciate instances of supernatural moral value—a humble man or a charitable man, on fire with love for God and his fellow men. These instances possess surprising glow and powerful attraction. They enrich the natural banquet with their supernatural quality. Third, the man may grasp that these instances *are* "instances"—that is, that things that are immeasurably greater than the instances can be found by meditation, namely, the inexhaustible exemplars of all the values, natural and supernatural.

We may picture a man as hiding behind a post. He has watched the once darkened banquet hall become filled with glowing, surprising, individual goods. But now there is a great hush. The concrete realizations of all the values, although they are quiet at the table, seem to strain themselves to point to something far greater than they. The exemplars of justice, humility, and charity can be concealed no longer: in their pure brilliance, they dazzle the man. For an instant he sees each as the true and inexhaustible Source of all the concrete realizations. He sees Justice alone, as fountain from which all just deeds spring, and Charity, as fountain of all realizations of charity on earth.

But an even greater joy and surprise awaits him. He sees the separate lights of Justice, Humility, and Charity begin to converge. In the next moment, the Infinite Person of God stands before the man. He shines with unimaginable splendor, clothed with all values. So far as the banquet, as such, is concerned, no greater good can become explicit. All greatness and goodness, all splendor, all beauty, all values are seen to flow from the inexhaustible Source, the One God. All perfections which were but implicitly known when the man of reason discovered that a personal God exists are now explicated, thanks to faith. The instances which in themselves had delighted the man are overshadowed by their exemplars. And these are seen rooted in one Supreme Reality—God.

The banquet now is fully spread. But we must use our other distinction if we would complete our analysis. For this banquet is not available even to the man of faith, except on condition that he make a great *effort* in recollection and meditation. Suppose, thanks to some special power, that a man might someday enjoy this banquet with no effort. Suppose the great source of all values, the person of God himself, were someday to be present to the man *face to face*. Should we not say that in this case an even greater banquet happiness is possible than in the case of a man of faith on earth, who must make such great efforts even to peek, as it were, at the great banquet table? The increased richness would be due, as we have noted, not to any new value of the object but to a new ability of the subject to touch the object in all its depth and plenitude.

We have at last reached the absolute climax to all banquet happiness. It consists in this: that the inexhaustible Principle of all values, fully explicated, is self-present to man, so that man needs no effort of recollection, for he just as easily and vividly grasps God as, now, he can grasp his beloved spouse on earth. If ever this should happen to a man, we may be sure that no higher banquet happiness is possible to him. He shall be seated at the table of the Infinite Person, fully explicated and truly present "face to face."

The reader may recall that a climax to banquet happiness is by no means identical with an absolute climax to happiness as such, taken in all its forms. Even with respect to happiness that is motivated by human persons, banquet happiness is only the first level. The second level is reached when we experience *love* for the values that are spread out before us. So too with the Divine Person. Though we sup at this *beatific banquet* with perfect rapture, though we be thoroughly warmed and caressed by the infinite beauty and loveliness of God, though the charity of God pierce us through and through, we have yet a new level of delight in store. This shall come when we love God, when we experience within our spirit a soaring, outrushing love, when we tremble with love before the Perfect Beloved. A third and still greater level is possible when we find our love requited.

We must apply to the second and third levels of happiness the distinctions we used to analyze the first level, the banquet happiness afforded by God. For our love can be toward the God that the man of reason knows or the God that the man of faith knows. Again, our love can be for a God who can be grasped by us only with much effort, through recollections and meditation, or else for a God who is self-present to us. We can say, therefore, that as the banquet becomes richer and more explicit—above all, as the banquet becomes at last self-present to man—man has the objective possibility of loving to a greater and greater degree. To the extent that he *does* love, an unspeakably great happiness will join itself to the loving, a happiness above and beyond that of the banquet happiness. He will experience joy, swelling from his depths—joy creative and soaring as he loses his heart in love for the Perfect Beloved.

We need not go through all the stages of this second level; let us be content to notice its absolute climax. A man shall experience the highest and most intense happiness of loving when God is immediately present to him, fully explicit, radiating from himself the splendors of all the values.

From this climax of the second level, we need take but a short step to reach the climax of the third and last level, the absolutely highest happiness from every point of view. If ever man experiences it, it will be something like this. The Infinite Person, now not only a banquet for the spirit but also the Precious Beloved, the One the heart yearns to be with, the One whose presence gladdens the heart—this Person will slowly turn his head in search of the man who loves him. He finds the loving man at last, there—hiding, smitten with love, filled with delight to feast on the splendor of God and to feel love for God pouring from himself. And now the breathtaking moment: the Precious One *sees* the man, learns of his love. The glance, the stare of the Infinite Person is now fixed on finite man.

Like a ray of white light, which contains all beautiful colors, that glance of God toward man will involve an entire spectrum of meaning. Although the glance, with all its different significances, will be accomplished in some kind of eternal fixity, we may separate some of its features and review them one by one, as if they form a temporal succession. In the first place, the man will be *known*. The secret subjective being, the inner personality of the man, will be the *object of divine knowledge*. What is fame in comparison to this? Who would seek the fame that a blurred multitude of humans can give when he has the genuine experience of being known by the One who counts?

Second, the white light of God's glance will carry God's *paternal praise* to the man. The Father, the beloved Father, the Precious One, will praise the man! "Well done", the glance will say; "You are known by me and I praise what you are; you have succeeded in the only real sense of the word: you have fulfilled the vocation of man, to be good." To hear these words, to be told he has succeeded, to be praised by God! The man who is thus blessed would melt in humble joy. This could never be interpreted as a subjectively satisfying joy, as if the words appealed to his pride or some subjective need. No, this is the supremely important example of genuine self-involved happiness. The metaphysical root of the man's existence, his true subjectivity, his real self, would first be known, then praised! We might say that from the first moment of his existence the man had no other goal, no other objective destiny than that moment when the Author of his being should *accept him*, should praise his subjectivity, should approve of his person.

Third, God's glance will answer the burning question with which the man at first approached God. He has nursed a great love for God and is bursting to declare his love and beg for its requital. He asks himself the great question: "Does the Beloved One love me? Is my love for the Precious One requited?"

The same glance, burning with love, says "Yes!"

Now must the spirit of the man overflow with such intense, in-credulous joys that it will seem too weak to contain them. This is the absolute climax of happiness: requited love with the infinitely preci-ous Beloved Person, with God! No further joys can be conceived or demanded, since no further joys are possible.

Chapter 7
The Ideal of Happiness

We have thus far surveyed the various kinds of experiences which are able to bestow a positive consciousness on us, whether caused or motivated, whether value motivated or subjectively satisfying or self-involved. We have also established what the absolute climax of happiness would be. All this makes it possible for us to conceive the essence of perfect happiness, the idea or ideal of happiness. We are not concerned whether the ideal is realizable in fact. We simply ask: if by some divine favor a man should be given perfect or ideal happiness, exactly what would such happiness consist of?

This much we can immediately put down: the state of ideal happiness would exclude all misery, whether of body or spirit, and even all chance and threat of misery. For if there is a man who does not endure misery, a man who is surrounded by beauty and beloved persons, the man is not perfectly or ideally happy so long as the loss of the things that make him happy is a possibility. Thus of two men, each presently happy, the one who has no fear of losing his happiness is closer to the ideal than the one who grasps, however implicitly, that the very jewels of his content and joy are threatened daily by a thousand possible thieves that lurk in the shadows of temporal existence, whether wars, or crimes, or sickness, or perfidy, or—above all—death.

That worry and concern, or "care," is a real enemy of happiness is exemplified in act V of the second part of Goethe's *Faust*. Four gray women, personifications of want, guilt, care, and necessity, stand before a house whose gate is bolted. Three are barred from entering, but the fourth, Care, boasts: "Your entrance, sisters, is blocked by bolted gates, but I slip in through the keyhole."

Our ideally happy man, therefore, has at least this negative happiness, this freedom from all misery and all threats of misery. What a blessedness this is, to be exempt from the stings of bodily hurt and spiritual woe! But it is only the beginning. Positive joys must now move into the neutral consciousness. Concerning these positive joys, we must make the following remarks. First, ideal happiness need not include any joy that is based on illusions or perverted viewpoints, for these are but sickly substitutes for the genuine joys. A man who is truly happy, who is filled with the bliss that genuine values afford him, would be indifferent and even hostile to illusory goods that might clamor for his attention. Thus the strictly subject-motivated joys, based on goods which are totally or partially illusory, likewise the joys of being known by the multitudes, of being famous—above all, the malicious joys that spring from things which flatter our pride—all these are contrary to the spirit of ideal happiness. That now they are so strongly desired, that most men are satisfied with these illusory and perverted joys alone, is a tragic indictment of the pitiful and sickly status of the human race. How truly wretched are men that they thirst for the pseudo joys of fame; that, even worse, the self-imprisoned joys of hate and envy should attract them and mold their personalities!

A second remark is that, though the ideal of happiness excludes all joys that are based on illusion and perversion, it by no means excludes *lowly* joys or joys that are based on modest realities. The temptation is to think that if one has the higher, one does not need the lower. Thus St. Augustine says: "He who has God and nothing else has as much as he who has God and the whole world." This is no doubt true. In a real sense, the higher obviates the *need* for the lower. But a genuine ideal of happiness must display all real joys, high and low. If, later, we admit that a man who possesses the highest happiness by this very fact possesses *per eminentiam* all the lower ones, we at least shall know exactly what it is which he no longer needs.

Let us begin our synthesis of the ideal of happiness. We may start with those subject-motivated sources of positive consciousness which are not illusory in whole or part, namely, benefactor achievement and knowing, considered as a flexing of the mind. The extent of the joys afforded by the first is appreciated if we think of all the situations in life in which we can do something good and experience a legitimate, warming joy when we become aware of our achievement, and still avoid any boasting or self-glorification. The joy the intellect takes in itself when it "flexes" before concrete beings or types has already been discussed; here we need only add that ideal happiness will demand the fullest possible flexing of the mind, so that every one of its potencies is actualized. We must stress, however, that this subject-motivated joy which comes from using or flexing the mind is not the same as the object-motivated joy which results because the mind responds to the splendor and depth and value of the known object.

In addition to the subject-motivated joys (just mentioned), the ideal happiness must include joys which can come to us from subjective sources of two general kinds: from innocent, legitimate, subjectively satisfying goods or from self-involved goods. Insofar as mere subjective needs are concerned, we must say that their satisfaction, strictly speaking, is but a negative happiness, for it is painful to experience needs. When they are satisfied by the *minimum* object they crave, the negative pain is replaced by neutrality. Thus all subjectively satisfying "happiness" which consists in the satisfying of needs, whether bodily or mental, is included in our first broad condition for the ideal happiness, namely, freedom from all misery and all threats of misery.

The case is different, however, with goods that are the object of wants. These "luxuries" for the subject, provided always that they dethrone no value (neither the value of the person's dignity nor any morally relevant value in the world), are no doubt to be included in the ideal happiness. Not that each must be actually enjoyed, for we have noticed that certain high goods may contain lower ones *per eminentiam*. Still, for the body to be caressed by innocently obtained goods, for example, is a source of positive consciousness for the person. Notice that this experience concerns a *caused* positive consciousness. Thus a good wine and a tempting steak are enjoyed by a man. The causal reaction between the objective qualities of wine and steak produce a positive feeling in the man, even as, on the contrary, tannic acid or soap would cause a negative reaction of distasteful, unpleasing flavors. Now the caused positive consciousness does not remain strictly enclosed within the bodily sphere. After a delicious meal, the whole person "feels good." A great sense of contentment is evoked by the pleasures of the palate. The spirit expresses its mild but genuine joy in being surrounded by luxury and bounty. Our ideal includes, then, all innocent goods that satisfy and favor subjective wants.[1]

The ideal includes goods on a higher level—those that deal with self-involved happiness. It belongs to the ideal of happiness that a man be known by another person, that the other pierce through and reach the man's subjective being, and that the knowing one praise and love what he knows. Provided the other really knows, and he is competent and sincere, his act of loving the subject assures the latter of his own inner preciousness. His praising the subject climaxes what genuine self-love really seeks: to guard one's preciousness and to let it flourish.

We cannot overestimate the importance of such self-involved happiness. Though it is by no means the basis of all happiness, it brings the person a special dimension of joy which otherwise would never be experienced. For all the while a man is free from misery, all the while he is bathed in the pleasures of goods that satisfy innocent wants, he remains *isolated*—a cosmos unto himself, but essentially lonesome. Not even values allow him to shatter the isolating sphere of his loneliness. For all the while he feasts at the banquet of values, he remains isolated, even though he experiences great joys. The isolation is broken only when another person comes upon the scene and casts his glance on the man. The latter feels that he is watched, that *his own subjectivity* is now the theme of a situation. How truly wonderful and joyous if this subjectivity should

/ See *Ethics*, chapter 7, where von Hildebrand shows that the subjectively satisfying goods can be considered as objective goods for man, and, moreover, that the latter situation has a value of its own.

please another! What a real success a man is if his moral superior praises him! This joy of existing within the knowledge of another, of being the object of another's admiring, loving glance, is of its own kind, and cannot be substituted by any other joy, however profound.

Our ideal thus far includes the following: perfect negative happiness, that is, freedom from all misery and threat of misery; the subject-motivated joys of benefactor achievement and of knowing as such; the enjoyment of all innocent luxuries of body and mind, the self-involved joys of being known, being praised, being loved by another person. Add now the three climaxes of happiness discussed in chapter 5 and the ideal is complete. Thus a man must sup at a banquet of values, then he must love the goods that are endowed with values, and finally, he must have his love requited. Each of these three climaxes has an inner progression of its own and each progression finds its high point in the reality of God. Hence *perfect* or ideal happiness would demand that the banquet be ideal, the beloved good be ideal, the requiting love be ideal. What else does this mean than that the full splendor of the values of God be present at the banquet table, that God be loved with all the soaring that such a value can motivate, that God himself should love the man as well as know and praise him?

Is it not astonishing that our minds can grasp this ideal, can understand that it is indeed the ideal, even though we have never experienced anything close to ideal happiness? We do not propose to discuss the epistemological question of how it can happen that a man knows more than he experiences; we content ourselves with noting the fact. For it is an evident fact that we really *know* the ideal of happiness and that we measure our slight approximations to the ideal by comparing them to the ideal itself. Thus whoever suffers is eager to be rid of his sufferings. He grasps that of two men, the one who suffers is further from the ideal of happiness than the one who does not suffer.

Again, whoever loves a human person finds that the values of his beloved are genuine indeed and profound—but not the last word. Something essential is grasped as being absent, some hidden value is dimly perceived as that alone which is big enough to activate every last fiber of the heart in loving it. The oft quoted words of St. Augustine are most relevant here. "Thou hast made us directed toward Thee," he half complains, half exclaims in delight to God, "and our hearts are restless until they rest in Thee." Man again and again verifies the truth of this remark when he loves great values which are yet finite (e.g. other humans) and discovers that his love is not yet the ideal—not yet what love *should* be or even *could* be.

A most important conclusion follows from the above summary of ideal happiness and from the observation that we know something that is better and higher than anything we have ever experienced. The conclusion is this: man on earth is condemned to move between the ideal of happiness, which is somehow always present, and the reality of earthly life. The latter has many joys, but they are far from perfect: many values for its banquets, but never the ideal value; many beloveds, perhaps, but never God in his presence; many requitals, but never from the Perfect One. Above all, life on earth has many miseries, and always the threat of misery. Man thus is *taunted* by this double knowledge of ideal and earthly reality. Had he not even a dim grasp of the ideal, he would not be so restless. When good things come, he would enjoy them. When miseries come, he would suffer, uncomprehending but resignedly, like a wounded animal breathing heavily and awaiting death (or a slow cure by purely natural results). On the other hand, if man truly experienced ideal happiness, all the secret desires of his true subjective existence would be fulfilled and his heart would sup at a perfect banquet, would love the Perfect Beloved, and that love would be requited.

But earthly life offers neither the experience of ideal happiness nor the "blessed" ignorance which would keep the slightest hint of ideal happiness from man. As we have said, earthly life offers this painful, taunting contrast between what *could be, what should be,* and what *really is* on earth.

With our analysis of happiness in general, crowned by our synthesis of what constitutes the ideal of happiness, we have brought to explicit consciousness the truth that must torment every man: his life on earth from time to time allows glimpses of a silver and gold ideal of a paradisical existence in which his heart, free from all oppressing evils, enjoys the highest happiness, but when it comes to granting him *experience* of the ideal, his life on earth is unyielding. It is man's lot to see but not to touch, to desire but not to have the desire fulfilled, to know but not to experience.

Exactly which features of earthly life frustrate the realization of ideal happiness are the topic of the following chapter.

Chapter 8
Enemies of Earthly Happiness

Now we must outline the best in happiness that life on earth can offer a man and then ask what prevents this happiness from being even close to the ideal discussed in the previous chapter.

Let us sketch the image of a man who is actually happy. He is healthy. He works either in a profession which involves a steady but pleasing exercise of his spirit (e.g. a mathematics professor or curator of an art collection) or in an interesting trade (e.g. an electrician, shipbuilder, or plumber). He lives during a time of peace on the international scene and prosperous, tasteful living in the local world around him. He fell in love with a girl when he was young, and she requited his love and married him. He and his beloved wife are still deeply in love; each is a source of enchanting joy to the other. They have three normal, healthy children, obedient and charming, whose innocence and youthful sincerity enrich the already rich lives of the parents. The man has several good friends who enjoy certain beauties in art and, of course, nature, and he often has the opportunity to be among (and appreciate there) beautiful things.

Does this man enjoy a happy existence? Few would deny that he does. His face bespeaks contentment and joy. His eyes twinkle with warm delight. Others, especially the wretched ones of the earth, look on his happiness and think: "If only we could have even one-tenth of the happiness that man has!"

If it be objected that we have deprived our happy man of certain goods which earthly existence might afford, we answer by giving the objector permission to make whatever changes his reason suggests as desirable in synthesizing the highest happiness that is possible on earth. Our point is that whatever is painted as a full or final picture of earthly happiness—however strong and complete—it will nonetheless prove inadequate against the enemies we mean to introduce. Let the objector give free rein to his imagination. Let the happy man have all the "extras" that anyone deems necessary. Let the objector add or subtract what he will from our sketch of the happy man. We will then pose our original question: Does this happy man, as so conceived and imagined, enjoy ideal happiness? Is he as happy as a man could be in a final, absolute sense?

The answer, obviously, is in the negative. The best existence on earth can not even approximate the ideal, as two general considerations will prove. First, life on earth, even at its best, carries with it inevitable miseries, sorrows of great moment. Second—on its positive side—it is not at all what the ideal calls for. We shall discuss the first consideration first.

The very fact that a man loves his present state of happiness, enjoys the things that are responsible for it—the very fact, in short, that life is good— implies that to lose this good life is not good, hence evil. Death of self, therefore, is not simply a formidable enemy to earthly happiness, it is *the* enemy, the only foe that is unconditionally to be feared by the happy man. It cannot be bribed, coaxed, restrained. It may perhaps be put off for a while, but it will not be cheated of its prize. Death does not merely threaten the man, as an army might, only to be diverted by some chance occurrence; death categorically *claims* the man. It is not simply a threat, not a bluff, but a factual claim which no man can hope to evade. Only the exact time is hidden when the claim must be paid. But the claim itself is never hidden, never really unknown by a man.

The happiest man, nonetheless, sings in joy as he greets the dawn. He is healthy and vigorous. He melts with happiness as he sits down with his beloved wife and beloved children—all of whom constitute the jewels—the beings—who give him happiness. During blessed days, weeks, perhaps years, he may be imagined to laugh and sing and delight with his precious beloveds. Apparently, there is not a shadow of unhappiness in the bright ambiance of his joy. But wait. A shadow has all along been present, though hardly noticeable. Little by little, it begins to lengthen. Soon the man grasps that he grows older, that the end of his bliss slowly but surely approaches. He begins to grasp this sorry fact when the parents of his friends die. How unexpected, how shocking! How wrong that they should be torn from earthly life, just when they have retired and are about to enjoy extended leisure and peace.

Then his own parents die. He realizes how useless it had been to hope for something different. They too were mortal and hence subject to the loss of life. But they were of the previous generation, which, after all, is thirty years older. But now one of his friends dies, who was his own age. At last he sees what perhaps he had resisted all along: regardless of what generation a man belongs to, *he too must die.*

What does death mean for this man? A blessed peace? A quiet, dreamless sleep? Let us reflect: the man is, by hypothesis, *happy* on earth. Death, therefore, can mean none of these pleasant, quietistic things. It can mean only that he who dies is stripped of all goods. Losing his life, he loses all!

Without doubt, the man has all along experienced genuine earthly happiness. He continues to do so. But now the ideal, shining as brightly as before, begins to taunt him. "Perfect happiness," it seems to say, "would involve the continuation of bliss. Bathed in joys, surrounded by beauty and precious beloveds, you would each day experience the ecstasy of loving and being loved, of living fully amid the treasures of life. But your happiness is far, far from this. Though intense, though perhaps enduring for forty, even fifty years, it is doomed to end. You stand to *lose all*—your life, and with your life all you have worked to possess, and all beauty, all loving, all being loved."

To those few men who squarely and honestly face the inevitability of death, death is rightly grasped as the great *tragedy* in earthly life. Merciless, it cuts down the happy man and takes everything away from him. While he lives and is happy, he cannot but say "Yea!" to life on earth, cannot but "affirm" existence and find it good. But then, if he is honest, he cannot but be touched with deep sadness, a lonesome, bewildered sorrow as he watches the shadows of death lengthen day by day and serve notice that they will certainly enclose him in their dark silences.

Not all happy men have enough courage to notice death. Consequently, they take great pains to be distracted, to have all morbid thoughts swept away by entertainment and various diversions. (We shall consider such tactics in the next chapter.)

We turn now to that other class of men, undoubtedly the majority, who do not and cannot look upon death of self as a great tragedy, or even as something sad and fearful. They are told that death has claimed them from the very start, that—ultimately—they too will lose all when death actualizes its claim. They sigh without emotion and say: "By then we shall welcome death; we shall have had enough of life, with its joys and sorrows." They mean, of course, that they shall have had enough of *sorrows.*

Let us reflect on their attitude toward death. Their secret longing for an end to consciousness or, if not this, their implicit welcoming of the slayer of life—their nonchalance, even their wry smile—when they are reminded of the impending arrival of death, testify to one simple fact. Considered as a whole, with good and bad parts weighed, life on earth is a burr in the heart, a misery, an experience that is best ended. For decency's sake, perhaps, they will cloak their disappointment at life with generalities. They will say, for example, that life has many good points—that they are happy that they at least embarked on "the great adventure of life." They will conclude, however, with something that is closer to the truth, which their heart knows; they will say: "But now the adventure is about to end, and we are not sorry."

With this remark they convict life of being, overall, a negative experience. For if its good parts made up for the bad, then life would mean something precious, something to be cherished. This is evidently not the case with these men. Their hopes have been rudely crushed, their desires frustrated. They have had many years of discontent. The few happy years of their life demanded many more years of misery as payment. Whether spousal love, or family life, or fame, or discovery of truth—whatever the good that brought them happiness—it also brought tiny serpents of misery. Most of these serpents matured and injected their poison. No matter the reason, life has somehow come to mean a bad bargain, an experience that charges outrageously for a few happy moments and, simultaneously, continues to taunt its luckless "customers" with shop-window displays of unlimited, perfect happiness.

This brief consideration of the fact of death of self teaches the important truth that life on earth falls badly short of ideal happiness. No matter what deep joys it may bring, it is very far from the ideal. Rather, it is much closer to tragedy. For either a man truly enjoys earthly happiness for forty or fifty years, and death means that he loses all, or a man finds life on earth so dull, so miserable, so disappointing that death is welcomed as a merciful agent which will snuff out a worthless, suffering consciousness. Is the first alternative not a tragedy, that the soft and fragrant blossom of happiness be not simply despoiled but utterly destroyed? Is it not in every sense a tragedy when a man looks upon the beautiful things of life, upon precious beloveds, and is forced to say: "I must depart forever from all these"? And is it not an even more pitiable tragedy if a man does *not* find death sad? Is it not much sadder to think that this exalted consciousness, this person, has found life so evil that he welcomes its end?

Death of self is the greatest enemy to earthly happiness, in the sense that it cuts the roots of all temporal consciousness and destroys all further chance for earthly existence. It is not, however, the greatest enemy in a qualitative sense. In fact, when a man is reminded that by death he loses all, he sometimes consoles himself by the plausible thought that "at least I won't exist to worry about my loss." Thus he argues that death of self is not a real tragedy, not a real sorrow, because the only person who might look upon it as such is the very person who (by hypothesis) no longer exists. (We have, of course, deliberately suppressed any religious convictions about immortality and all religious links to supernatural reality, for our concern is to show what life on earth really means to a person without religion.) To return to our former point, we say that although a man fears death as the end of his happy life of earth, he can console himself that, when death comes, he will no longer feel anything, or suffer any pangs of loss, for the simple reason that he will no longer be.

What, then, can be considered the real qualitative antithesis to a happy earthly life? Death of self, as we have seen, means only the absence of happiness, at least from the nonreligious viewpoint, which hopes for no immortality and fears none. The answer is simply this: a happy existence is *changed* into a miserable existence, without destroying the consciousness which experiences the change. This change is what really attacks earthly bliss, since it forces the formerly happy person *to survive* and bemoan his loss, to continue to live, but with burrs of sorrow and miseries of every kind. What can change happiness to misery, joy to sorrow? We answer: the death of loved ones, the irrevocable loss of the very persons who motivated happiness.

Of course, the death of loved ones is not inevitable in a man's life. Surrounded by precious persons, a loving spouse, good children, a man may enjoy many years of bliss before he dies, and be *survived* by all his loved ones. Such a man escapes the misery of experiencing the death of those he loves; he suffers only the sudden ending of a beautiful life—his own. He was not required to live while his jewels were stripped from him one by one; rather, he was forced to take leave of them. They remained his until his last light of consciousness was extinguished.

Although it may happen, therefore, that a man escape the misery of losing a loved one, such escapes are rare and improbable. The happy man has at least one person (usually more) whose life and health are the basis for his happiness. Let one of his beloveds—his wife, for example—be stricken by some illness, let her linger between life and death, and the man's joy gives way to fear, concern, hope, helplessness. Now let the beloved die. Wave after wave of bitter, forlorn, tormented, sobbing sorrow perturbs his spirit. The last parcel of joy is driven out and replaced by sorrow. What does it matter that other precious beloveds remain? They cannot console the bereaved man. They cannot replace the unique jewel that was taken away by death.

More probable than the death of his wife is the death of his parents during a man's lifetime. Of course, if the man did not love his parents, if in fact he disliked them, their death moves him to no sorrow, no concern. But in this case the man was not as happy as he could have been. For if his parents, dead, move him to no sorrow, it is because when his parents were alive they were no source of joy to him. Thus he is not as happy as the man who gets on well with his parents, who loves them and is loved by them, so that their loss is deeply felt. Here again we find the basic law of happiness on earth clearly indicated: to the extent that life itself, or some good thing that is given to us in life, rejoices us, to that extent does loss of life or the good thing sadden us. To the extent that the loss does not sadden us, to that extent were we lacking in happiness during the time we lived or had the good thing. Who, understanding this law, dares contradict it? What philosopher can explain away its implications, what witty epigram can laugh them away? Life on earth stands convicted of being very imperfect, very far from the ideal.

We must go further, however. Although death of self spells the abrupt end to all earthly happiness, and is unique in this respect, the death of loved ones is by no means the only antithesis to earthly bliss. We must see that other qualitative enemies to earthly happiness exist. It is foolish to blame the death of loved ones for all misery. A hundred lesser agents, all bent on slaying happiness and replacing it with misery, are concealed in every life. So efficiently do these agents work that scarcely a man lives to be sixty, who still retains a love of life and thinks of death as his only fear. Perhaps he once loved life, and then death was his greatest enemy; but the lesser agents have soured the milk of happiness, have slipped scorpions into his heart. So now, at sixty, he says to the once feared death: "Come, claim your prize."

He is perhaps not entirely sincere or clear-sighted, or single-minded, in this yielding attitude toward death. In his consciousness is a deeply rooted ontological affirmation of being and a corresponding dread of total annihilation. In all subhuman living beings this elementary dread of death is openly and naively exhibited. But in man it is often ignored, suppressed, distorted, and sometimes even overcome. Nevertheless, it is sufficiently operative in most men that they will endure all sufferings and sorrows (with only one or two exceptions) if only they remain alive. Though it is easy to speak about death in a casual way and with bravado, it is much more difficult to face the thought of total annihilation squarely and remain calm. To be no longer—to have one's personal life not merely changed, but wiped away—to sit down today and reflect that tomorrow one will have fallen into nothingness, totally and irrevocably. These are somber thoughts. Pressing always from the depths of consciousness, they provide strong reasons to dread death and to look with horror upon the possibility of ceasing to live and ceasing to be.

Despite this elementary dread of death, however, a man may find few reasons to have a positive desire for life. As mentioned above, lesser agents crowd in on the man and war against his earthly happiness. They wear down any positive love of life that once may have existed, with the result that the man finds himself between dread of dying and dread of living.

What are these lesser agents that war against earthly happiness? First, we may mention crippling sickness of all kinds and the loss of sense organs and limbs. The once erect human body is suddenly cut down, its splendid surfaces ravaged by ulcerations and diseases of all kinds. Its integrity is damaged by loss of sight or hearing, by amputation or atrophy of arms and legs. Or it suffers a heart attack or the beginning of cancer. All crippling injuries, all prolonged and serious illnesses, are such that they ruin much positive happiness in life and yet, unlike death, promise no immediate relief from the miseries they generate.

We readily admit that sickness as such is not always a catastrophe and that a serious sickness often turns out to be a blessing for a man who lives on a high level. Many a sick man has discovered the seriousness of life—the reality of God, the fact that others love him, and so forth—*because* he took sick and was torn violently from a thoughtless, ego-centered existence. He then looks upon his sickness as a fortunate evil, because it brought with it an incomparably higher good. Nonetheless, sickness and crippling injuries need not always turn out so well. Just as often they embitter their victim, who wails pitifully at the sad discovery that his former joys are gone, crushed forever when his health collapsed. Life on earth becomes a long, painful wait for death. Many wretched persons try to shorten the wait by suicide.

Still another antithesis to earthly bliss is based on compassion for the suffering of others. If a man experiences pains or sorrows—if, therefore, he is the subject of a negative consciousness—we suffer in sympathy with the man (provided, of course, that we know of the man's distress and that we are not hardhearted). However, to feel sympathy for another's suffering is a negative experience—an antithesis to earthly bliss. How much happier we should be if there were no *occasions* for sympathy, if we looked all about us and saw happy, smiling persons. But such serenity is denied us. Even though we are filled with our own joys, when we turn from our private lives and look upon others we are touched by their sufferings of mind and body. We feel with them, and this no doubt consoles them in some mysterious way. At the same time, this sympathy means sorrow for us, where none existed before.

Again, if we learn of some objective evil that another person suffers, whether the other experiences it as evil or not, we pity the other. We sorrow not *with* him but *on behalf of* him. Such pity arises when we see blind, crippled, and mutilated persons, especially children. We also pity evil men who continue to damn themselves by their evil ways. Even though we ourselves are happy, we become afflicted with pity when we look upon the millions of persons around us, all of them incomplete and lacking in some respect or other. How much happier we should be if we lived amid *whole* men, strong and complete, clothed with health and moral integrity. But this too is denied the happy man on earth. Though he himself is happy, his heart absorbs the woes of others and becomes less carefree, more somber, even sad.

By now it should be obvious why no happy earthly existence can approach the ideal. For death of self is inevitable and known to be so. This knowledge continues to taunt the happy man, so that he never enjoys a good without somehow realizing that all enjoyment will be abruptly cut down by death. The death of loved ones threatens to turn joys into miseries. Sickness of self is able, and always threatens, to dry up many sources of earthly bliss. Finally, the sufferings of others constantly move us to sympathy and the objective evils of others move us to pity. Sympathy and pity, although they are good attitudes and in some cases are even morally good and perhaps obligatory, are nevertheless negative afflictions of the consciousness. We should be much closer to ideal happiness if no suffering and evil existed around us.

All this shows that, *even at its best,* earthly existence is far from the ideal happiness. We have seen, moreover (in chapter 2), life on earth is not often at its best—it is almost always much worse than its best. Scarcely a man exists who is not troubled by some burr in his heart; scarcely a person who enjoys even one year of uninterrupted joy; scarcely a person who has even one year free from misery of some kind. Anyone who looks objectively upon our planet must be struck by the incontestable fact that earth contains great oceans of miseries and sufferings and, only now and then, small islands of joy. And even these islands are daily threatened by towering columns of ocean—are already condemned to be washed away after some little time.

What man would defend earthly existence as enjoyable, or as more enjoyable than miserable? He would be convicted of error: first by the almost universal misery of the human race and then by the potential miseries that will certainly befall even those few who are relatively happy. The Church has well called earthly life a "valley of tears."

Chapter 9
Facing the Problem of Evil

Only a few men take an explicit stand on earthly existence, its opportunities for happiness, its overall worth, and so forth. Most men live from day to day, from problem to problem, from hope to hope. At most, therefore, they have only an implicit world view of happiness on earth and a never-really-formulated plan for achieving whatever it is that their world view suggests is attainable. A few men, it is true, try to think through an explicit solution to the problem of man's quest for happiness. These are the philosophers. Their reasoned theories are soon found in the marketplace, where they form the core of some implicit "solution" to the problem of trying to live a happy life.

This problem, in its essentials, is based on the flagrant contradiction between the ideal of happiness, which is dimly understood, and the reality of misery or threatened misery, which is vividly experienced. How shall a man respond to earthly life, with its excesses of sorrow? What must a man say when he is taunted by the ideal, which mocks him as he undergoes miseries?

In this chapter we shall survey three general ways of answering or facing the problem that the reality of evil poses for the happy life.

131

They are compromises in action, compromises in theory, and pessimism.

Part 1: Compromises in Action

We can proceed in an orderly way if we distinguish, first of all, between what a man suffers in his experienced encounter with the evils of life and what position or attitude he thereupon adopts toward life and the evils it is known to contain: in other words, the specific collision with evil and the subsequent reaction or counterattack. Now this reaction admits a very important subdistinction, for it may be that it is an "escapist" position and therefore basically dishonest, since it evades the foe it is meant to attack. Or it may meet the fact of evil squarely as do all honest positions vis-à-vis evil. (Needless to say, a position which is honest, in that it does not ignore or evade the evils of life, may be false in that it answers evil with false or distorted convictions.)

A man's encounter with the evils of life may be gradual or abrupt, may follow upon a neutral consciousness or a positive consciousness. In the end, the effect is the same: the man is weighed down with suffering, pains, sorrows, indignations, and so forth. His subjective existence, his precious individuality, is tormented. He is buffeted from many sides and pricked and stung. Participation in war, death of a beloved spouse, unrequited love, the burden of some great guilt—any of these might have introduced him to the evils of life. How does this lived encounter with evils affect him? In every case, this much at least happens: the man undergoes the torments of a negative consciousness. He *feels* the barbs and burrs that are inflicted on him by the evils in question. More may happen, however. The man may be unable to bear the weight of pains and sorrows which assail him, in which case he will succumb to madness. Madness does not fall under what we have termed a reaction or counterattack; it belongs to our category of what a man suffers in his lived encounter with evil.

Let us reflect on this fearful effect that is inflicted by the evils of life. The rational consciousness of the victim is unable to endure the nightmarish world of reality. For reality means evils, and these mean suffering; and suffering means days and weeks of the same sickening, despairing consciousness. Thus, as if to preserve *some* part of the person, his rational mind flees the world it can no longer endure. How pitiable is this state, which is nonetheless intelligible. For madness can be a defense against too-great suffering— somewhat analogous to fainting which mercifully puts the consciousness to sleep when bodily pains become intolerable. The madness of King Lear is an excellent example of how too great a mental anguish inevitably *distracts* the mind, turns it from the real world, lest, remaining in the nightmarish real, it scream and wail in an agony it was never meant to endure.

A man's lived encounter with evils, therefore, implies that he suffers to one degree or another. If his suffering is so great as to be intolerable, he becomes mad. In this case he has no chance to make any reaction or counterattack. He cannot take a position toward evil for he has already been vanquished. Unless he is helped in a radical way, he rots away in his enslavement—a prisoner of war, captured by the evils of life. But suppose a man does not succumb to madness. Suppose his encounters with evil make him suffer but do not rob him of his sanity. What reaction will he take toward evil? What counterattack will he make against any new evils that might befall him?

We have mentioned a basic distinction in counterattacking attitudes (some are "escapist" whereas others are "honest"), and we shall treat the escapist attitudes first. Here again a distinction is needed, between escapist attitudes which involve a "drugging" of the subject and those which simply misinterpret various objects of experience. The first may be called "opiate" attitudes, since their aim is to divert the subject's attention from evils at all costs. The second may be called "Pollyanna" attitudes, since they are but shallow convictions that put forward a pseudo optimism with much noise and bravado.

Suppose a man's life to be a tortured sequence of sorrow, bother, pain, boredom, and worry. Day by day he looks upon a bleak, chilling dawn and curses the next ten hours or so that he will have to endure among his fellow men, perhaps in a job he detests. Pain and sorrow oppress him in a steady rhythum. What methods can be adopted to put his troubles out of his consciousness? For one thing, he can literally use drugs. During the hours when the drugs do their work, he is "blissfully" unconcerned about the evils that crowd in on him. Their fearful faces are somehow unreal, like masks, while the drug works its effect; their points are blunted and cause no pain and sorrow.

To drug oneself in this literal way is, of course, the classic "escapist" method (from which all analogous methods derive the appellation "drugs and opiates".) In this literal sense, the drug is a biochemical agent which attacks the brain centers and nerves and somehow keeps the person from experiencing what really affects him, namely, pains and sorrows. The true inner personal consciousness is put to sleep. Minimum peripheral consciousness is allowed to remain, and it is "massaged" and caressed by pleasant feelings and imaginations which swarm in to replace the negative realities of the person's real life.

A more ancient and more widespread form of escapism is drinking alcoholic beverage to excess. A man who has lost an important business contract, a lover who receives final notice that his beloved will see him no more, a financier who has lost heavily in the stock market—each may mutter, half in disgust and half in pain: "I'm going out to get drunk!"

The reasons for drunkenness are admittedly complex. We do not pretend that every instance of intoxication and all cases of addiction to alcohol are based simply on the wish to escape. On the contrary (especially in singular instances), the reason for overdrinking may well involve festive joy or overenthusiasm. Nevertheless, a good proportion of excessive drinking can be traced directly to the ability of alcohol to effect a temporary escape from evils. Besides the millions of people who consciously "drown their sorrows in drink" and get intoxicated as often as troubles seem too great, millions more are motivated not by any single sorrow, consciously grasped, but by a general weariness and disgust with life. Often they are lonely and dejected, and they are never happy. Drinking means they can escape from unhappiness for a little while.

Another method of escaping the awareness of evils is to use

"drugs" of the mind, which operate quite differently from drugs in the literal sense. The latter attack bodily processes and yield a *caused* relief; the former operate through knowledge. They "charm away" sorrows and worries through their message for the spirit of man. Thus the man who is afflicted with suffering can *daydream*. He soon learns the trick of ignoring the present reality and attends to the imagined possibility. When he is adept at daydreaming, he resembles the insane person. Both men focus on an unreality which is not unpleasant; neither turns to the reality which means suffering, because it is evil.

The insane person, however, has no choice. His "critical breaking point" has been reached and his madness is thus a "necessity." Not so with the daydreamer; he *chooses* the dream world as more pleasant. However, he could endure the unpleasant real world. He therefore is to the insane man what the literally drugged man is to the fainting man: the insane man and the fainting man are powerless to endure more, whereas the daydreamer and the drugged man prefer pleasant unreality to distressing reality. No doubt, the latter two can become habituated to their drugs so that they are "necessities." But prior to this addiction they took the drugs as a matter of preference, not necessity.

A second form of mental drugging is less drastic than daydreaming. It consists in feeding oneself a steady diet of "entertainment." This method has certain marks of sanity that are not found in drug addiction or daydreaming, for the person finds his consolation and escape in the *real* world. However, he ignores those parts of the real world which are distressing and concentrates on a few superficial parts which keep his mind busy without burdening it.

The most obvious form of entertainment drugging is that in which the person is passive. He "absorbs" cheap novel after cheap novel, "sensational" books one after the other. He is forever focused on trivial pursuits. He seeks "interesting" plots in the second-class books he reads and scandals and gossip in the daily papers. In recent times, he views television indiscriminately for five or six or more hours a day and supplements it with "action" movies and "comic" and "girlie" magazines.

A steady diet of "entertainment," such as we have described, is by no means similar to "relaxation" in the sense of a genuine need of the mind. For relaxation means turning from the abstract to the concrete or from the practical to the nonpractical. Relaxation, therefore, need never imply turning to sensational novels, or gossip, or "hit" television shows. These things, it is true, may also allow one to relax, since they deal with concrete and non-practical affairs, but as a *steady diet*, they cannot be considered relaxing in any sense, for the person who so indulges himself obviously has no time for anything to relax *from*. What matters here is the quantity. Low-level entertainment, if only occasionally enjoyed, may well equal relaxation, but the latter need never imply low-level entertainment. If it is steadily enjoyed, such entertainment is a drug which diverts the consciousness from its problems and "charms away" sorrows and worries with it dulling, soothing powers.

Thus we see that two different motives can underlie a person's stuffing himself with entertainment. The first is the desire to escape from his troubles; in which case he seeks a negative "happiness." So long as the person's attention is diverted, he does not feel the boredom, worries, and sorrows which afflict him. The second motive is positive. A steady diet of entertainment not only diverts attention from the person's suffering, it also yields pleasant experiences. It flatters his concupiscence. He is pleasantly thrilled and excited by the sensational novels, the gossip, the complex plots, the scandals, and so on.

Entertainment drugging also has an active form. As we have seen, in its passive form it means the person continuously *absorbs* things. In its active form, the person goes out and *does* things. If such a person is a man, he races sports cars, collects stamps, chases after women, enthusiastically "follows" a ball club, and so on. If a woman, she may keep a spotless house, attend the "best" functions, organize poetry circles, and join political organizations. Now all these actions of the man and the woman are not, as such, drugs. They can also be forms of legitimate relaxation, and even genuine value responses. However, when a person embraces all or some of them with an exclusiveness that amounts to idolatry—when, for example, he looks upon racing sports cars as the *chief* thing in his life *and as something that really matters*—he makes a drug of what might be harmless relaxation. Thus the spending excessive time on them and overvaluating them entitles us to call such things drugs.

What was noted about passive drugs applies equally to these: they yield the negative happiness of diversion from misery and the positive happiness of something that is subjectively satisfying. In this case, however, the subjective center, which is flattered, need not be concupiscence, for pride may be the underlying principle which renders such active entertainment attractive.

So much for the first kind of things serving the escapist attitude, which we have termed "opiates" since they drug the consciousness, whether through caused processes of the body or motivated processes of the mind. We turn now to the "Pollyanna" escapist attitude, which is characterized by a falsification of experience so as to create a pseudo optimism. In general, it is based on denying, mitigating, or overlooking some great evil—death and sin, for example. Whereas the honest, objective attitude is to regard such things as evil, as fearful realities which are reason for concern, the Pollyanna attitude talks them away or shrinks them to insignificance. This attitude appears most often as an uncritically held prejudice which interjects itself into concrete experiences of evil. It sometimes appears, however, as the reasoned result of an allegedly critical investigation. Thus we have two forms of Pollyanna optimism, which we may call the "popular" and the "philosophical." We shall treat the popular form now and reserve discussion of the philosophical form to part 2 of this chapter.

The "popular Pollyanna" is a man who has a smile, a witticism, a slogan, or a neat cure for every evil. Remind him of death of self, show him it is inevitable and even imminent, and he answers with a witty reference: to "St. Peter," "pearly gates," "harps," "devils," and so on. He tells you he has always wanted to see what's "up there," that he'd like to meet the "Great One," if he exists—that in any case, even if he goes "down below," he will have the consolation of meeting all his friends again. The great mystery of death, the staggering loss it entails for man, inasmuch as it strips him of everything—these facts are not considered by the popular Pollyanna. He enjoys his witty references to death too much.

When pressed to be serious, he becomes sentimental and almost nostalgic about death. He says it will mean that he "goes home at last," that he will embark on "a great, thrilling journey." He continues to misunderstand death, of course, for he completely misses the point that death may mean a day of wrath, a day of terror, when his subjective existence will be scrutinized in truth and judged good or evil.

His attitude toward the death of loved ones is equally superficial and flippant. Remind him that his beloved parents will soon die, or that any happiness he enjoys with his wife or children may suddenly be torn from him by their death, and he answers that one can't expect his parents to live forever, or that his "better half" will be better off without him, and he will wish her Godspeed when she is about to die, or that his children, if they die, will escape a life of hard work, and—anyhow—he will meet them again in a "better life."

All these allusions to another world, a better life, and so on would be praiseworthy if, first, they were meant seriously by the speaker and, second, they were based on something more solid than sentimental whims—for example, if they were based on belief in revealed religious *truths*.

For the miseries of other people the popular Pollyanna has not jokes but slogans and "cures." Of the impoverished wretches who cover most of the earth, he thinks all they need is "a good dose of self-reliance," or "some training in mass production," or "more democracy." About sin in general, whether his own or others, he thinks people "make too much fuss." "Live and let live," he says.

Life, therefore, seems good to this man. Death and moral evil hold no terror for him. His self-induced joviality, he soon finds, is welcome in superficial circles, where it brightens the gloom or boredom that threatens to settle over the group. Of course, when real evils strike close to this man, he is stunned and speechless, badly confused, and even desperate. But after the initial shock he reverts to his joviality, which perhaps is even emptier. But no matter, his slogan continues to be "Laugh and the world laughs with you" and "That's what life on earth is for, isn't it—to laugh and have a good time and keep away from gloomy killjoys who are always haranguing the world about death, evil, sin, God, and the like?"

That this popular Pollyanna, whom we have only briefly sketched, indulges in escapism is easy to see. Though not drugged, either literally or mentally, he avoids the reality of evil and even the depth and seriousness of good things. He is therefore uncomprehending when one talks about the miseries of life and the truly sad contradiction between the known ideal and experienced real. He feels sure that he is having a good time and that everybody else can have just as good a time "if only . . ." In a sense, he has reduced his understanding of good and evil to that of an imbecile.

Part 2: Earthly Optimism, the Theory of Compromise

Perhaps the most persistent and far-reaching form of escapism from evil is not the use of drugs or excessive entertainment or carefree and thoughtless popular slogans but highly sophisticated and allegedly critical philosophical theories about happiness which we may group together under the general term "earthly optimism." It is indeed surprising that a philosophical theory, which has the single mission of laying bare reality as it is, should instead gloss over much that is important and almost all that is unwelcome. Yet this is exactly what is done by most earthly-optimistic systems of "ethics."

In this part, therefore, we mean to examine the core of this optimism and show how it conspires (far more than drugs and popular slogans) to throw a veil over death and all the mystery and sorrow that are linked with death. With death comfortably disposed of, it proceeds to write a slick program for happiness. This, in turn, deludes all who espouse it and results in the scarcely believable fact that many students and specialists in philosophy are more blinded than their unthinking, unsophisticated brothers to the evils and sorrows of life. Their philosophical theory insulates them from lived experience and renders them senseless and dull to the drama, and then to the nightmare of living on a planet where death slays personal consciousness.

Generally speaking, the earthly optimist is rather satisfied with the way life treats him. Because he has thought much, his philosophy gives him a sense of power, a sense of being "above" the mass of men who struggle for existence and for scraps of contentment and joy. With a mild sigh, he realizes that, unfortunately, not all men enjoy his serenity and well-balanced view of things, but this is because most men are silly or weak enough to allow themselves to be duped by nonsense, rhetoric, superstition, and the like. Life is really not fearful or miserable; at least it *need not be*. We humans, he writes and thinks, have a chance for a very interesting and useful life of fifty to seventy years on a very exciting planet. So many pleasures and joys are offered us, so many zestful activities, so much beauty and charm, so many chances for love and friendship. Let us then partake of what life offers and not bemoan our separation from the unattainable infinite.

"Be satisfied!" is his charge. Do not poison the good things of the present by contrasting them with absent better things, if the latter are unattainable. On the other hand, be dissatisfied with things that can be bettered. Use your intelligence to remake the world at hand and mold it nearer to your heart's desire.

Should a person fear death? Of course not. Make up your mind that life and you have formed a bargain. For fifty years you can have a tolerably good time. Then you will be asked to yield your place on earth and lose consciousness forever. What good can there be in resisting the terms of this bargain? At least, make sure you are not cheated of the fifty good years. Go ahead and live!

The earthly optimist, we see, is not at all happy about the actual state of affairs on earth. He really sees evils: injustice, broken homes, wars, and so on. But he thinks that no evils are inevitable and that a dose of "reasonable living" can straighten out society and individual men. From the start, he neutralizes a truly inevitable evil, such as death of self, by calling it not evil but a fact of life, the limit and one of the terms of the bargain.

Again, though he is distressed by many evil actions and attitudes of man, such as theft, murder, hatred and envy, he mitigates their effect. He does not interpret them as morally evil and, therefore, of great moment (as Macbeth interprets his evil actions); he does not think of them as violations of any ethical imperative. No "Thou shalt!" thunders out to man from a voice beyond man. If an attitude or action is viewed with disfavor by the earthly optimist, it is because it is antisocial or foolish; the former when it tends to frustrate the happiness of others, the latter when it ruins the happiness of self. The "problem" of ethics (if any part of ethics remains) becomes an inquiry into a "calculus of pleasure or happiness" of the self alone and then in a society of other selves. If pleasure rather than well-being or happiness is stressed, we have hedonism, instead of eudaemonism. However, these two theories agree in the important respect that both are based on earthly optimism.

Earthly optimism thrives in any antimetaphysical atmosphere. Denying or ignoring any reality beyond time, it quickly comes to terms with time. It puts the limits of man's existence at birth and at death. Only the interval between these limits counts. Western positivism is very fertile soil for this worldview. Indeed, some brand of earthly optimism has been held by every important British positivist from Hume to Bertrand Russell; in America, it is perhaps found most completely in the naturalism of John Dewey. It tacitly identifies the *ethical* problem with the problem of the "happy life" on earth. In effect, it distinguishes fools from wise men, the latter being those who see the whole picture of life on earth and suit their actions to an overall program of self-perfection and enjoyment.

The "good man" of earthly optimism is the one who employs "reason" or "intelligence" as instruments of amelioration. The "happy man" is the one who lives a rich, fully integrated satisfying life—and then dies.

What else is this optimism but a subtle form of escapism? We may imagine some youths who rush to positivism or naturalism with terror in their eyes, fear in their heart. Death has cut down their parents and loved ones, and continues to threaten them and make a mockery of all their possessions. How does one face up to death? How does one dispel the dark shadow it casts in the courtyard of earthly happiness? What advice does a wise philosopher give concerning inevitable evils? "Forget death! Take the realistic position that life ends with death and that nothing you do or think can change this. Resolve to act intelligently so that you, in the years remaining to you, can become more perfect, can actualize many of the potencies of a man. This is your good: to be more fully a man!"

How easily are youths persuaded to lose sight of the ultimate problem of death. Instead, an intelligible and attainable goal glitters before them: to savor new dimensions of experience and to actualize their potencies—to have their manhood flower, to become more perfect. What makes it especially difficult for youths to realize that their original questions have been parried and avoided is their feeling of superiority when they contrast their newly found attitude with the desires of the vulgar masses, who seek "sense pleasures" or, worse, follow an otherworldly will-of-the-wisp, served up to them by a discredited, unscientific, medieval institution. These youths, however, now that they have been converted to philosophy, have put their intelligence to work in pursuit of an earthly goal that can actually be reached, and without "mystical" intonations.

They are thus immersed in an escapist position, since it avoids the question of the evils entailed by the death of self and loved ones. They are equally confident that theirs is *not* an escapist position, since it was adopted only after long, critical study; since, above all, it is based on a "realistic" appraisal of life on earth and existence in general. Thus they are caught by the strands of an invisible net which is slack enough to allow some measure of freedom and thereby nourishes the illusions that it is not there.

All philosophical theories of earthly optimism are open to at least two basic criticisms. The first is directly to the point and easily grasped: an alleged theory of a plan of happiness which tacitly ignores death, which dresses up death in whimsical garb, or introduces death and quickly expels it from the discussion room, is—really and fully—an escapist theory, founded on a gigantic illusion. To push death aside, the most momentous reality of human life, and blithely chatter about happiness and serenity is hopelessly superficial. It is a procedure worthy of those who are gripped (as Pascal profoundly observes) by a kind of "supernatural enchantment."[1]

---

1. One merit of Heidigger and certain other serious existentialists has been that they force the learned world to stare at this momentous datum of death. Happily for the truth, philosophy now tends to be "death conscious."

Our second criticism rests on more subtle grounds. To understand it, we must distinguish the theory of happiness from the theory of ethics in the strict sense. The first has the primary task of telling us what happiness is and the secondary task of saying what we ought to do if we want our share of happiness. For over a thousand years, this question of happiness had been identified with "ethics" or moral philosophy. Gradually, however, this hypothetical "ought" of happiness was distinguished from the unconditioned, categorical "ought" of morality. Philosophers achieved a fully explicit grasp of the unconditioned "ought." They pointed to a basic datum of man's life on earth, clearly grasped in some instances, that certain things *ought to be done*, others *ought not be done*. The "ought" is grasped as binding unconditionally. One *ought not* slander one's neighbor, even if one can do so with impunity. One *ought* to respect just laws, even if no advantage follows. One *ought not* murder, even though one is prepared to accept the punishment meted out to murderers. The *ought not*, as well as the *ought*, still binds, regardless of objective consequences—regardless, too, of how the agent subjectively views these consequences.

It is entirely possible, therefore—in fact it is necessary—to elaborate a theory of ethics without asking the question "What leads to our happiness?" In fact, only when the "ought" of morality is considered by itself, apart from any reference to happiness, is it possible to grasp the true nature of morality. However, we do not mean by this to deny that a deep link exists between morality and happiness. On the contrary, once we grasp the nature of moral goodness, we see that it calls for a reward, which can only be happiness, even as moral evil calls for punishment—for unhappiness.

Socrates saw this link between morality and happiness when he said, "It is better for man to suffer an injustice than to commit an injustice." In other words, a man's happiness is hurt less by his receiving an injustice in moral innocence than by committing an injustice in moral guilt. This insight of Socrates, however, does not erase the need to consider the question of moral "oughtness" on its own, without reference to its consequences for happiness. For the question of what is unjust or just, morally evil or morally good, can be answered only by consulting the morally relevant data. It would constitute a vicious circle, sterile and misleading, to try to understand moral goodness in terms of its consequences, as "that which calls for happiness." Unless we understand moral goodness "on its own," we cannot appreciate that it calls for happiness.

Kant brought the distinction between categorical and hypothetical oughtness into such sharp focus that we now recognize an ethics in the strict sense, whose task is the elaboration of goods that are relevant to *moral* obligation—to the unconditioned "ought" of morality. Of course, prior to Kant, the "ought" of morality was always implied in every moral code, above all, in the Ten Commandments. Moreover, such philosophers as St. Augustine and St. Anselm based much of their ethical theory on an implicit grasp of the distinction.

It is of the utmost importance to keep this distinction in mind. Much harm has been done to the theory of ethics by confusing it with the theory of happiness. Moreover, the theory of happiness has been distorted and falsified because at times it has been conveniently identified with ethics, when it suited some author's purpose.

We, on the contrary, mean to keep the two theories distinct. We insist that the theory of ethics is independent of the question of happiness, since the former can and must establish the ground of the unconditioned "ought" without reference to happiness. As we have stated, the "ought" of ethics binds whether we desire happiness or not, whether or not happiness is objectively linked to a proposed deed. Any theory of ethics, therefore, has the task of discovering what is morally good and obligatory and not "what leads to happiness." A theory of happiness, on the other hand, must worry about happiness and misery when it surveys the various conditions of life. Unlike a theory of ethics, a theory of happiness has no right to *avoid* questions that are directly related to happiness.

With all the above as preface, let us proceed to our second criticism of earthly optimism. This philosophy, whether espoused by the British positivists, or by Dewey, is really concerned about the happy life for the individual self. The wise man, the reasonable man, will so arrange his life that, first, it yields the most happiness for the effort involved and, second, it somehow does not interfere with the chances of other persons to live a happy life. Let us now notice what follows from this. Heroism, any fighting to the death for what one holds right, all efforts to overthrow evils at the risk of death, all such actions are foolish and ought to be discouraged. For given that I follow this earthly optimism, why should *I* risk my life to save someone who is drowning? Why, though innocent people are threatened by evil invaders, should *I* fight against the invaders?

The answer must somehow fit in with *my* happiness. The earthly optimist is not allowed to slip in an ethical "ought" or such words as "noble," "heroic," "good." Granted it is noble, heroic, and good to try to save the drowning man, to fight off evil invaders—but how does this add to *my* happiness? What possible happiness can come to me if I *die* in trying to save the drowning man or fighting the invader? Of course, if I survive, my life will be richer, more "rewarding," etc., because I can bask in the thought of how much I have helped others. But if I die? How foolish to expose oneself to mortal danger for a reward which can never come, since I will not be alive to enjoy it.

Our second criticism therefore boils down to this: earthly optimism must consistently discourage as foolish anything which involves heroism and risk of life. It must even be wary of condoning heroic acts that are made for the sake of beloved persons. A mother who risks ruining her health to save a child's life during a long sickness; an aging philosopher who spends long and hard hours writing a book he does not need; a physician who goes to a leper colony to minister to the afflicted, at great risk of contracting the disease; a missionary who goes to a savage nation to teach it religious truths, as well as scientific and civilized practices in social and hygienic customs—such persons excite the admiration and respect of all unprejudiced people. What they achieve, what they attempt, is noble and stirring—yet all of them are convicted of foolishness by an earthly optimism that is logically consistent. Because it puts the totality of existence between the limits of birth and death, it must find the justification for all "good" actions between these limits. But when the deeds which stir men, because the deeds are noble and heroic, result in causing the death of their agents, no part of the agents' life span (between birth and death) persists in being, so as to vindicate or somehow justify their sacrifices.

This criticism does not apply to a genuine *ethics* of action which recognizes the clear call of values and teaches that one *ought* to respond to certain situations, not for the sake of any expected happiness but because the situation itself is endowed with an inner preciousness, a value, which calls for cooperation. Earthly optimism *is not* an ethics in this sense. It tolerates no categorical obligation; it brushes aside all talk of values objectively existing *in* objects and situations. It reduces the ethical question, What ought to be done, what avoided? to a foreign but easier question: What ought I to do in my years on earth if I want to get the most out of them? This is the question which underlies all earthly optimism.

We have criticized such theories of optimism not *because* they treat earthly happiness but because, when they allegedly treat such happiness, they *avoid* the absolute threat to it, death. Their basic flaw from our standpoint (which is limited to a critique of happiness theories, not ethical theories) is that they rest on an escapist theory of happiness, which is founded on the gross illusion that death can be mitigated or ignored when one treats of a "realistic" plan of happiness.

Part 3: Pessimism as an Honest Solution

We have seen the various escapist answers to the problem of evil on earth. We have looked at some of the chief opiates, bodily and mental, which dull the mind and thus insulate it from the palpable evils of life. We have seen the popular Pollyanna attitude, which avoids the miseries of life with wisecracks, slogans, and the like. We have seen finally, the philosophy of earthly optimism which constructs a theory of happiness within the limits of birth and death and thus dismisses death from the problem as "irrelevant," and mitigates moral evil so that it seems like a temporary nuisance which is about to be overcome. Now we turn to attitudes which squarely face the fact of evil and, therefore, are called "honest" rather than "escapist."

The honest attitudes toward evils on earth fall into two large classes. The first comprises those which see the evils as inevitably triumphant and which teach, in consequence, a doctrine of pessimism in an ultimate, strict sense. The second class is a single attitude, which, facing all the evils of earthly existence, looks upon them as inevitably vanquished; it sees them as "redeemed" and somehow neutralized by a good that far outweighs them. This attitude alone deserves the name "genuine optimism." It does not avoid facing evils with the pseudo optimism of the Pollyanna. It does not honestly face evils only to admit defeat, as in pessimism. On the contrary, it *sees beyond* real evils to a good that inevitably is victorious.

This genuine optimism belongs exclusively to the Christian attitude toward existence. Because of its unique basis, we shall devote the final chapter to outlining the Christian worldview. The remainder of this present chapter will deal with honest pessimism.

We note that, in general, every theory which faces evil squarely tries to come to terms with it—does not try to avoid it, as escapist theories do. All forms of pessimism, therefore, are alike in two basic respects. Each sees the real evils that are an inevitable part of earthly life, and each, shrinking in horror from these evils, devises means to counteract them. It follows that one system of pessimism differs from another chiefly in its means for resisting or otherwise encountering earthly evils.

Perhaps *cynicism* is the most radical pessimistic answer to evil. The cynic[2] sees two facts clearly. First, each man will suffer in life, no matter how he tries to avoid it; second, the chances of miseries are multiplied a hundredfold by any positive happiness a man may enjoy, for each time he takes a step upward into positive consciousness, he risks a more fearful fall into misery.

The cynic has a sad but logical answer to these two facts. Since all

---

2. We use this term, and later the term *stoic*, to refer primarily to philosophical *types*. These types roughly correspond to historical schools but do not necessarily agree with these schools in every respect.

positive happiness is pregnant with misery, which will, when it strikes, be far greater than the happiness, man should resolutely *shun* positive consciousness, even all hope and desire for positive consciousness. Let man so despise all the dazzling "goods" of life that he can count them as nothing. To attain this conviction, he must reflect that these "goods" demand too great a price. In exchange for a short and never perfect joy, they will exact a long and profound sorrow. One laugh must be paid for by a hundred tears.

The cynic, then, wants nothing to do with positive consciousness. Moreover, he wants as little as possible to do with negative consciousness as such. What best consoles him, what he really desires, is *negative happiness*, which means "neutral consciousness." Since this is only an ideal, he considers himself fortunate if he approximates the ideal.

As has been often remarked, *stoicism* is incomplete and insincere cynicism. Like the cynic, the stoic is primarily concerned to arm himself against misery. He seeks to achieve perfect serenity of mind—such that not a ripple of emotion, positive or negative, will disturb his neutral consciousness. To the stoic, neutral consciousness is the supreme good, which is what he means by "apathy." However, whereas the cynic's desire for apathy makes him consistently renounce the *actual* enjoyment of goods, the stoic, inconsistently, seeks to retain and enjoy whatever comforts, pleasures, and joys come his way. At the same time, he tries to discipline his spirit into regarding these goods as dispensable luxuries. He strives at all times to be "above" every situation. The stoic thus wishes to enjoy actual goods, and in this respect his life can be happier than the cynic's. Also, he wishes to arm himself against possible misery, if ever his fortunes change and his goods are replaced by evils, and in this sense he is like the cynic, who also seeks the least misery.

We may summarize each position by saying that the cynic wants apathy through perfect renunciation of all positive consciousness, whereas the stoic has the double-minded hope of enjoying positive consciousness while remaining *detached* from the "goods" that bring it about.[3] The cynic's life can be perfectly consistent and

---

3. This "detachment theory" plays an unfortunate role in many Christian ascetical works, which have been greatly influenced by Stoicism.

successful, even if very sad in its despairing attitude. The stoic's life, on the other hand, is a living contradiction, for no man can simultaneously enjoy a good, be detached from it, and be ready to lose it without the least regret or discomfort. This is true even of minor goods, such as pleasures of the palate and the comforts of good living. It is especially true of major goods, such as beloved persons.

What father is stoic enough to enjoy his son, be happy in his son's presence—and suffer no sorrow and regret if the son should die? Above all, what man can taste the bliss of requited love with a precious woman—and not sorrow when he loses her, through death or necessary parting? That the historical Stoics were aware of the insufficiency of their double-mindedness vis-à-vis apathy is evident: they recommended suicide when misery became insupportable. This can never be necessary to someone who is truly apathetic— except, perhaps, if he were about to face bodily tortures and pains (against which no amount of mental discipline or philosophy is of much avail). But if torture and physical pain are excepted, there should be no need for suicide if one has "achieved" genuine apathy, for he would be untouched by the death of beloveds, the loss of fortune, the perfidy of friends, and so forth.

It remains for us to touch briefly upon the most famous pessimism in Western thought, that of Schopenhauer, and, incidentally, upon its Eastern matrix, the pessimism of Buddhism. Schopenhauer is rightly celebrated as the most eloquent spokesman in the West on the miseries of earthly existence. He had the merits of intellectual honesty and powerful exposition, and because so much of what he wrote concerning misery is true—because all he wrote is so forcefully and brilliantly expressed—his works have become a haven of resigned gloom. Today, in accelerating retreat from various forms of pseudo optimism, of escapist solutions that have been tried and found wanting, many men are wont to return to the caves of Schopenhauer's pessimism. "If it is not consoling, it is at least true, and that is something," they seem to say.

Like his Eastern masters, Schopenhauer looked upon the finite personal existence of man as a great mistake, as the result of some metaphysical blunder or disharmony—even as a crime, as *original sin.* He supported this extreme view by observations that are as true as they are commonplace: let anything good appear and soon it is killed, or twisted, or tainted. Hopes are dashed to pieces, noble aspirations are condemned to frustration, more and greater evils are unloosed by each further evil. All of men's strivings for earthly happiness are vanity, for death and sickness, accident and change, wars and the perfidy of others work against the smallest beginnings of joy.

> This is the state of man: today he puts forth
> The tender leaves of hopes; tomorrow blossoms,
> And bears his blushing honors thick upon him;
> The third day comes a frost, a killing frost
> And . . . nips his root,
> And then he falls
>
> *Henry VIII*, act 3, sc. 2

Seeing the madness, anguish, and absurdity of so much that passes for earthly life, Schopenhauer looked sadly at the futile process of finite existence and said, in effect: "Ah, if only this had never been! If only the pains and anguish, the wails and screams, the pitiful state of man and all living things, if only all these could really cease—or better, if only they had not been in the first place!" But it is real, this world of misery and tears. Man cannot think it away; man is forced to stare upon an objective world of great beauty and wonder, a world which promises so much, while his subjective world, his own consciousness, his spirit, is torn with a thousand sorrows, great and small, or with boredom, or with unsatisfied, gnawing desire for things that are not present. Thus mocked by an elusive and taunting joy which never is possessed and, meanwhile, undergoing real sorrows and pains which are as real as joys are unreal, what shall man do? Not to have been would be best—but this is impossible. The next best thing is *relief* from misery, and perhaps even *salvation* from misery.

Relief is possible only for intervals. The subjective world of anguish and sorrow, bitterness and frustration, can be momentarily quieted by focusing upon some great and beautiful *object*, a drama of Shakespeare, an opera of Mozart, Cervantes' *Don Quixote*, beautiful buildings, etc. All the tormented sinews of self-consciousness will be unflexed for a while. The subject will pay less and less attention to himself, more and more to the object. At last he becomes *pure knowing consciousness*. What a blessed relief! To be rid, temporarily, of the nagging desires and sorrows of self-consciousness! To see, if but for a short while, all the miseries of the world somehow neutralized and redeemed when they appear as objects *sub specie aeternitatis*.

But relief means *just* this. It is no cure. How does one *cure* the disease called living? What is the way of salvation? Schopenhauer's announced doctrine of the "denial of the will to live" is admittedly based on the Buddhist doctrine which exhorts men to achieve nirvana—a state of mind totally exempt from striving, hoping, desiring, cherishing, and the like.[4] Man must "empty himself," must *renounce* all satisfaction and even all claims and hopes of satisfactions. When, at last, by dint of asceticism, a man's will to live is slain, his consciousness is mercifully removed from the torment of striving and suffering. He is now at rest. Nothing can ever touch him.

Few are "heroic" enough to renounce life—but these few alone are "saved." The many who fear pain, desire relief, hope for better days—all are destined to subjective torment. Nor can they end it by suicide, which, since this springs from *affirmation* of the will to live and to be happy, cannot solve, but can only postpone, the problem of existence.

Schopenhauer wrongly identified this "renunciation of the will to live" with Christian asceticism. He insists that at least "primitive" Christianity taught this doctrine of renunciation. It is a well-known and indisputable fact, however, that no such renunciation was preached by orthodox Christians of any century. From the start, those who follow Christ empty themselves *in order to be filled with Christ*. Christian asceticism has never been seen as the way of salvation, which, because it kills every striving, brings peace to the soul. On the contrary, it is seen as a first stage (and a negative one at that) in the transformation of a person in Christ. Christians are exhorted to "put off the old man"; that is, to discipline those centers in the self which insist on self-affirmation and satisfaction, the centers of pride and concupiscence. They are then exhorted to "put on the new man"; that is, to nourish and enlarge their value-responding center within the "framework" of Christ, through the merits and help of Christ, and *with* Christ. The goal of all this is just the opposite of nirvana. It is the fully *positive* consciousness whereby genuine love—charity in the only true sense—will burn brightly in the heart and radiate its warmth and goodness to all objects in the universe. What is more, all natural goods are seen at last as rooted in Christ. Instead of renounced, they are enjoyed with a new purity and freedom.

Schopenhauer's theory of salvation is concerned, as he admits, with *negative happiness*. In fact, he thinks that only misery and pain are real. Their opposites, joy and pleasure, are simply the absence of suffering, which is real. He never grasped the difference between a neutral consciousness, which enjoys negative happiness *because* it is neutral and so is relieved of all misery, and positive consciousness, which consists in the *presence* of some delightful positive feeling, such as joy, love, enthusiasm. His goal was to be rid of misery, to be "happy" in the only sense he could allow—that is, free from trouble. Quite consistently, then, he advocated a way of "salvation" which is a kind of extreme cynicism. By "heroic" and absolute renunciation of all possible goods, a man will at last be liberated from all the miseries that attend frustrations of hope, unfulfilled desire, and so on. In a word, man's precious subjective existence, his real self, which aspires to what it thinks it should be and have, must be shown the error of such aspirations and must be denied a further chance to speak or to be. When the self is thus crushed and broken, when it no longer engages in even legitimate affirmation of existence, then at last it is free from all misery. It enters Schopenhauer's version of nirvana—something close to negative happiness (i.e. mere neutrality of consciousness).

Whereas the cynics and, of course, the stoics had but an earthly plan for avoiding miseries, Schopenhauer's plan is all-embracing. He means to give an *absolute* answer to the absolute problem of the fact of existing. Like the cynics, he faces the fact of misery squarely. His remedy, following his diagnosis, is more extreme because it is more absolute. In the end, however, all these honest attitudes toward evil betray a sickening despair which is only afterward covered over or "redeemed" by the various tactics advocated: whether by arrogant denunciation of positive joys, as with the cynics, or by ascetic renunciation, as with Schopenhauer and his Buddhist masters.

Let us summarize briefly. Evil is a fact and all men sooner or later encounter this fact. If evil proves too strong, madness separates consciousness from the evil reality, lest it totally destroy consciousness. If a man survives his encounters with evil, he may adopt either an escapist position toward evil (explicitly or not) or some honest position which faces the fact of evil squarely. In the first case, he will employ opiates or Pollyanna slogans or illusory worldviews of earthly optimism. In the second, he will look upon the world with despair in his heart and then, reluctantly, embrace what seems to him an acceptable answer to the unavoidable fact: some version of cynicism, stoicism, or renunciation in the Schopenhauer-Buddhist sense. But if he is honest in facing evil and if he does not despair, but hopes for genuine happiness, this is only because he has embraced the one genuine optimism, the Christian worldview.

Chapter 10
The Christian World View as Genuinely Optimistic

Part 1: Introduction

Our concern in this chapter will be to exhibit in outline the Christian world view insofar as it bears on the question of happiness for men. We shall not argue that the Christian religion is the true religion, for this is not a philosophical question. We are interested simply in the intelligible link between happiness and belief in the full Christian revelation. We intend to show that the man who believes in Jesus Christ as God, the man who cherishes in his heart the Word of God, the man who worships God in the manner that Christ ordained—this man has a well-founded reason to be optimistic about life on earth. This Christian optimism, as will be evident, is completely removed from all pseudo optimism, which is based on escapist attitudes and tricks. Squarely and honestly, it meets the facts of evil—so much that it can go into deeper depths of pessimism than ever Schopenhauer dreamed of. But it rises from these depths with the victorious, glorious conviction that all evil will be somehow

overcome—somehow even used for good things—which will more
than compensate for the evils.

To appreciate this worldview, which is based on belief in Christ,
we must begin with an analysis of world views in general. After
several important facts are uncovered we shall turn to the specifically Christian world view and elaborate its grounds for being the
only genuine form of optimism.

Part 2: World Views and a Personal Absolute

When a man looks upon his life on earth in isolation from everything else, he may be said to be adopting a "physical" view of life.
Good and evil, joy and sorrow, pleasure and pain—all are real and
meaningful to this man. They all, likewise, bear an *absolute* character. For the physical view is limited to the temporal interval between a man's birth and death. Thus a year of joy, followed by
another year of misery, is just that. The joy was something real that
passed away; the sorrow, equally real, takes its place. When the
man's life is over, the physical view can do no more than weigh the
"good times" against the bad to see whether the man's life was
worthwhile. During his life, the man would be expected to avoid as
much evil and gain as much joy as possible.

The moment may come, however, when a man is introduced to
the *metaphysical* aspect of life, at least to the problems and mysteries it presents—if not to any of the various solutions that different
systems of metaphysics offer. To be introduced to metaphysics, it
suffices that the man "step backward" and look at his life, not in
isolation but as related to certain undeniable realities—certain
forces or causes which are responsible for many events in a man's
life and even for his existence. At this point the whole theatre of
earthly life, with its good and evil times, its limits of birth and death,
is no longer seen as an isolated absolute but as related to other
realities, however dimly perceived.

The metaphysical view of man "locates" him within the totality of all things. Questions of origin and destiny become meaningful and personally important. The individual realizes that he is a point of consciousness, stranded on a vast shore, and yet is somehow related to other things within the limitless universe that surrounds him. He realizes, with some terror (or at least awe), that death need not be an absolute end, even as birth need not have been an absolute beginning. Realities existed long before he was born. One of them, or several in concert, acted in a certain way and he was made! More realities press on him even now, pulling him from instant to instant, and some day they will make his point of consciousness disappear from the world of time.

Various stages are possible in awakening to the full impact of the metaphysical question. If we make use of a myth, we can show these stages in clear outline. Let us suppose that a hundred men live together on a small planet which wanders in space. They are conscious of no motion, nor have they asked themselves how they got on the planet or where the planet is taking them, for each looks at the other ninety-nine and sees that they take everything for granted. They are there, they have been there as long as they can remember; the place where they stand isn't "going anywhere." Meanwhile they have problems on the planet: finding a comfortable place to sleep, growing vegetables for food, and so on. Economics (in the wide sense) is their chief preoccupation.

Now let one of these men step off the planet a little way and regard the spectacle of life from his removed position. How dramatic it seems: a swiftly moving sphere, climbing silently through dark spaces; ninety-nine persons, ninety-nine points of consciousness, huddled on that sphere. The observer now sees the *mystery* in the fact that the planet exists, that ninety-nine persons exist and meet together on the planet. He also sees mystery and drama in the destiny of these men and their planet. What force pulls them through space? Does it *know* whether it pulls them? What awaits them at the end? The observer, because he has "stepped back," is drawn into the mysteries of metaphysical questions. He has reached the first stage, which we shall call "awareness of existence." For so long as he merely existed amid other things, all of which existed—so long as he was right in the middle of existing things—he could not appreciate the profound mystery in the fact that anything exists. But now that he has stepped back, he becomes *aware* of existence as a reality of the first importance—which is easily overlooked, however, because it is omnipresent.

All alert, he scrutinizes his ninety-nine fellow men on the planet. He watches them for a long while. The mystery grows deeper: *new faces* appear on the planet! New persons, new points of consciousness, suddenly make their appearance. They speak and will and love and hate in their unique ways. As he watches, the mystery grows still deeper, even darker: an invisible force seizes one of the men and *pulls him off the planet!* He has disappeared. Our observer has reached a higher stage of metaphysics: awareness of *finite* existence thrown into a rhythm of time and suddenly pulled out.

He continues to watch, and notices something that had escaped his attention: screams and wails. At all times, some of the ninety-nine are writhing in agony or afflicted with great sorrows. Others prowl in the night and steal from their sleeping fellows. Some even kill their fellows. The planet, with its inhabitants, seems at once a great and thrilling drama and a horrible nightmare! Our observer has graduated to *awareness of good and evil.* He has reached that point in metaphysics which sees good and evil against the background of the totality of other things.

If the observer is allowed to return to the planet, he will tell the ninety-nine that their very existence is a great mystery; that evils, including death, threaten them; that it behooves them to get their wits together and form a defense against the evils by discovering the solution to the mystery of *being on a planet.* They will look at him as an "enthusiast" who has been frightened by a preacher or a science-fiction horror story. He, seeing the casual way they treat evil and death, may decide that his fellows are afflicted with a form of sleeping sickness, an enchantment which veils the real world and substitutes a fairyland of make-believe security and peaceful joy. In this case, he will remove himself from his fellows and, like Schopenhauer amid thousands of incurable pseudo optimists, will await with private dread his own doom. Or he may begin to doubt whether he is right and the ninety-nine are wrong. Perhaps his stepping back and looking at the planet was a foolish effort; perhaps what he thought he saw is of no real consequence. In this case, he will gradually dismiss his insight into the mystery of being as so much "metaphysical hogwash, which gets a man nowhere."

Let us assume that the man continues to take his insight into the drama and mystery of being seriously. Let us assume that he even resists any form of resigned pessimism and that he ceaselessly looks for some hint of an answer to the question of his origin, his destiny, his links to the totality of other beings. He is timid when he looks over vast spaces, and awed by the thought that millions of years may have washed over the patch of ground on which he stands. How strange and hostile and impersonal the worlds seems. There he stands, in the center of many infinities, on a cold sphere that moves through dark spaces. But now a glimmer of hope lights in his eye. His solitude, his fear before being, his sense of being surrounded by a hostile universe—these fears came because he looked first at himself and then at the very universe to which he is somehow related. But in this very relationship between him and the universe is his best hope for an answer! The very thing that awes him is the very thing that should console him: an Absolute exists—call it the One, or the Force, or the Universe; call it God, or Rah, or what you will. He is related to this Absolute.

For an instant the man knows hope and peace. For a single instant, the world makes complete sense; his existence is seen as sheltered by the Absolute. He breaks into a smile of joy and relief. He yearns to sing an ode to the Absolute, to that hidden Reality which cast him upon this strange but wonderful planet and which sustains him even now. In this instant the man enjoys the consolation of a metaphysical answer, however false, however improbable and difficult to comprehend. He sees the totality, eternally existing. He sees himself as clearly related to the totality. His small existence, his pinpoint of consciousness, rests like a fragile bubble on an immense totality. The man has found the Absolute, the only kind of being that can give an answer, even a false one, to the mystery of finite being.

But the man's hope is short-lived. His joy disappears and is replaced by a frown, and then by empty despair. For his Absolute is of no help; it is simply an *It*—of course bigger than the man, of course superior because eternal. But, nevertheless, only an *impersonal* something, and therefore *less* than the man. What an absurd Deity, which sustains persons but is only a Force, an impersonal Thing! This Absolute, which he had so eagerly embraced, because it sheltered his existence, turns out to be an idol, incapable of consoling breathing flesh and of no use at all in telling the man what *meaning* there is to his life on earth. The man smiles bitterly as he thinks to himself: "How deluded are men to pretend they find the 'answer,' and even the *consoling* answer, to the mystery of their being in an impersonal *Thing*, however vast and mighty. Let these men send cries of praise to their Thing. It cannot hear them. Their praises, pleas, their curses and blessings—all ring toward empty silence, are swallowed up by foreign spaces, and never does their Thing, their Absolute, hear even a syllable."

The Absolute, so conceived, is but a false dawn which cruelly mocks the man, who lives in his fearful, seemingly interminable night. But now comes the real dawn, now some incredible phenomenon begins to light the darkness. The horizon glows with a strange light: the man now grasps the *living and seeing God*, a Person! Like some cosmic giant, like some immense presence, this Person allows himself to be known by the man. Metaphysics now attains to a "personal absolute."

Many gradations are possible in a man's contact with a personal God. A man may *know* God as a Person, but may never engage *in personal contact* with God. As in banquet happiness, the man may hide behind a pillar, so to speak, and look out upon the splendor of a personal God—a being with consciousness, self-consciousness, will, affections. So far as knowledge of objective reality goes, the man has made the supremely important discovery. His mind has reached out and, somehow, touched the single important reality, a personal absolute: God. The man is dazzled by the immeasurable perfections of God, which are revealed to him piecemeal as he thinks about the "ground" of all finite existence.

No man can meditate on the Deity for long, however, without finding a great question frame itself in his consciousness. He scarcely dares formulate it, even silently, but it persistently suggests itself to him: "Does the Person know me? Is the infinite God *aware* of my existence?"

With this question unanswered, and seemingly unanswerable, the man continues to look at God, but with a sinking heart. What good is even a personal God if he is blind to the insignificant, finite results of his creation, if he is blind to man? What avails man all the great power and splendor of God if this God is deaf to the praises of man, the petitions of man, his pleas for relief from sorrow and for help of all kinds?

In this first stage of contact with a personal God, the man is perhaps cheered and awed by the objective splendor and majesty of God; but he is sorrowed by the realization that his finite person is so far below the infinite God as to be truly insignificant. The man realizes that if any "subjective" (i.e. person-to-person) contact is to be established, it can come only on the initiative of God.

Any higher level of contact with God must necessarily fall outside philosophy. Without exception, the history of philosophy affords no instance where a man claimed a subjective encounter with God. At first, of course, there was talk of revelation from the gods, from exalted and wise persons who were sometimes thought of as superhuman but never as infinite, absolute creators. Plato's admirable Book X of the *Laws* shows a philosopher's concern over the existence and characteristics of such superhuman deities, but he never suggests that these deities are personal absolutes, or that man engages in a two-way confrontation, a dialogue, with them. At best, the gods hear men and are concerned with the welfare of men; but men do not hear them. In the *Republic*, Plato attains a purer concept of God, in the sense that he looks upon his "Good" as an *absolute*, as the first principle of all perfection; but he is further away from a *personal* God here than in the *Laws*. Indeed, there seems to be a rule in philosophy that "personal" and "absolute" tend to cancel each other out, so that the more an alleged god is absolute, the less personal it is, and the more personal it is, the less is it taken seriously as an *absolute*, first principle. Thus, in the *Republic*, Plato strains to catch a glimpse of that reality, "beyond essence," which is

the fountain of all the splendor and perfections of the eternal essences and, subsequently, of all temporal approximations of the
essences. Plato's principle is not personal. On the other hand, his
personal deities in the *Laws* are not absolute.

Later philosophers claim to know more and more *about* God.
Never do they claim a subjective contact, person to person, between themselves and the Absolute Person. We may say, therefore,
that even in those cases where philosophers reach a personal God,
they never pass beyond the first stage of contact, for they know God
as *object*, albeit as a Personal Object. He is the splendid Presence as
seen from behind a pillar. He lives a transcendent life—a king surrounded by his court. And philosophers, even the best, are like
poorly clad beggars who climb steep walls to catch a glimpse of the
king, and then are forced to descend quickly, for their footing is
never secure.

Part 3: The God of Abraham

A completely different stage of contact with God occurs when
God initiates a dialogue with man, when God speaks to man. So
much is implied in the sentence "God speaks!" It means, first, that
God is a Person; second, that he knows about men; and, third, that
he addresses himself to men. Something comparable in philosophy
would be if Plato's "Good" were suddenly to show itself as personal
and were to speak to Plato as absolute Principle and Creator of finite
personal creatures. As we have mentioned, however, no philosophical absolute was ever grasped as a personal *subject*, and only a few
were grasped even as personal objects. But this new contact with
God is not reached by philosophy. What we focus on now is the
religious contact of the Jewish people with God.

In every way, the relationship of the Jews to their God is unique.
Unlike all the Oriental religions, the Jewish religion worships a
personal absolute, a Consciousness that is immediately linked with
every man in an intimate dialogue. A real dawn of hope and consolation at last appears in this Jewish situation. At last, a genuine reason
is given for a well-founded optimism: God exists, he cares for men.

He is good, he speaks to men. What can now hold man back from singing praise and thanksgiving for this central fact, this momentous truth?

> With expectation I have waited for the Lord,
> And he was attentive to me.

> And he heard my prayers and brought me out of the pit
>   of misery and the mire of dregs.
> And he set my feet upon a rock, and directed my steps.
> And he put a new canticle into my mouth, a song to our
>   God.

Psalm 39

No more is man a stunned wanderer, an isolated point of tortured consciousness. He is now drawn into the very center of the universe by his bond, his *religion,* with God, the absolute Person, the mysterious source of all being. The great evils of life lose their terrifying proportions when seen against the infinitely greater background of God.

> For though I should walk in the midst of the shadow of
>   death,
> I will fear no evils, for thou art with me.

Psalm 46

The personal Absolute of the Jews—"the living and seeing God," as St. Augustine calls him—is the key to any optimistic metaphysics. Given such a God, there is no longer any reason to bypass the problems of moral evil and death with dishonest evasions and escapist theories and attitudes. Nor is there any reason to face these evils honestly and fall into a deep and inconsolable despair. The life of man on earth is seen in a completely different light, as a chapter in a biography that began when God called each man into being, that developed in a series of temporal events on earth, that will find its explanation and fulfillment when God calls a man back to him in death. Everywhere the reality of God shines through, like an orange sun behind dull gray clouds. The knowledge that such a Person exists brings with it a joy never before imagined, much less experienced:

> O clap your hands, all ye nations:
>> shout unto God with the voice of joy
>> For the Lord is high, terrible:
> a great king over all the earth.   Psalm 46

Part 4: The Christian World View

The central dogma of Christian belief is the mystery of the Incarnation. This mystery says that the *same living and seeing* God, who is worshiped by the Jews—the same God who, somehow, addressed Abraham and Moses—this same God took on human flesh and human consciousness and, as a God-Man, walked the earth for thirty-three years. We stress that to hold this mystery as *true* demands faith, but that no faith is required to understand some of its implications. Accepted by the faithful as true, it becomes the motive of a new world view. We shall try to understand this new world-view insofar as it deals with happiness.

During the liturgical season of Advent, the Church reenacts the expectation of the Jews for the coming of Christ, their long wait for redemption, their hope for better days. God has already made known his existence, has already spoken to them. But he is still distant, and earth is crowded with evils, flooded by tears. Sin and death still mock all plans for earthly bliss.

> If only you would destroy the wicked, O God and the
>> men of blood were to depart from me!
>
>   Psalm 138

And again:

> ... but there is no one who pays me heed.
> I have lost all means of escape;
>> there is no one who cares for my life.
> I cry out to you, O Lord;
>> I say, "You are my refuge,
> my portion in the land of the living."
> Attend to my cry,
>> for I am brought low indeed.
>
>   Psalm 141

Still, the Jews hope:

> Behold, the Lord shall come and with Him all His saints, and in that day there shall be great light, allelulia [From Vespers in Advent in the old Breviary].

In one breathtaking *now*, all such prayers are answered and all hopes realized. On the first Christmas Day, the God-Man came into the world of time. So now, each subsequent Christmas Day, the Church proclaims the new theme of earthly life:

> By the mystery of the Word made flesh, from Thy brightness a new light has arisen to shine on the eyes of our souls, in order that, *God becoming visible to us*, we may be born upward to the love of things invisible.

The faithful center all their religious fervor on Christ. They meditate on the life of Christ, his deeds—from the first recorded one, teaching in the temple, to the last one, ascending into heaven. The faithful attend to the words of Christ, his teachings about God: Father, Son, and Holy Spirit—about sin and grace, about His role in their redemption. They attend, furthermore, to the *promises* of Christ—promises that the Spirit of God will abide with the faithful on earth, that unending happiness awaits those who love God and are obedient to his commands.

A totally new vision of life on earth is thus afforded the faithful. This strange planet Earth, beautiful but terrifying, has been sanctified by the real presence of God. God has touched the matter of this planet, has eaten of its fruits, has walked its paths. His very body has been formed of the matter of earth. So immediate and palpable a presence of God means that earth has not been forgotten or abandoned. Again, the faithful learn, and joyfully believe, that God loves all his creation, loves each created man with a "love that surpasses all understanding" (Ephesians 3:18). Each man is the beloved of God. Each is sought after by God with an ardent longing for requital. Divinity loves man and stoops low to be loved. Because God loves us, he desires our full and perfect happiness. He is really concerned that our subjective consciousness be filled to overflowing with pure joys, with ecstasies of delight; that all misery and threat of misery by removed from us.

The new, Christian vision make possible the specifically Christian virtue of *hope*. Hope transforms man's pilgrimage on earth, from a terrifying journey, without apparent purpose and with little consolation, into a meaningful period of trial *which will end in happiness*. The Christian faith does not erase or even alleviate the miseries and threats of misery in earthly life, but it *redeems* them by hope.

Hope in the promises of Christ quiets the anxieties of the Christian about the evil consequences of his sins. Hope, moreover, sees beyond the inevitable deluge of evils that affect the Christian as he goes from birth to death. Armed with hope, consoled by the real expectation of "good times," the Christian can afford to see earthly life in very truth. Perhaps he alone is fit to look at evil in *all* its horror and magnitude, because he alone possesses a well-founded hope that these evils will not triumph.

Others (as we noted in the chapter 9) are only too eager to avoid all contact with evil, to avoid even the mention of evil as evil. Even an honest pessimist such as Schopenhauer, however much he grasped certain miseries of earthly life, overlooked all the acute miseries that are attendant upon moral evil. He failed to appreciate either the horror of moral evil in itself or the misery that guilt brings to the evildoer. He noticed enough evil to make us admire his courage, however, and to wonder how he was able to support this vision of unredeemed and unredeemable misery within himself. He is clearly exceptional. Most men shrink from looking at a disease they cannot cure.

So our point is essentially true: only the Christian can look evil squarely in the face, because only he has a cure that is profound and potent enough to overcome its grievousness.

Hope calms the Christian as he looks upon the shortness of life, its dangers and its inevitable sorrows. In this, hope is an aid to negative happiness. St. Augustine says: "Were it not that we perceive the dim outlines of the eternal city, we should not be able to endure the misery of existence." Hope keeps our eyes fixed on a country not yet attained but attainable. We are able to count all the hardships and evils which befall us as minor obstacles in the path of our journey toward the "eternal city." Without hope, the hardships would seem too great—and, worse, meaningless.

Hope likewise functions on behalf of positive happiness. It tells the timid man, who is afraid of great risks because he fears great sorrows, to dare desire all the happiness he thinks possible, to dare look forward to joys without end—to perfect bliss. The Christian is urged to become a Daniel in his desires, to avow with full consciousness that he seeks nothing short of unlimited happiness. Hope makes a man bold, encourages him to admit to his innermost secret longings for real joys. The Christian who believes and who hopes is characterized by a restlessness for God.

> One thing have I asked of the Lord, this will I seek after; that I may dwell in the house of the Lord all the days of my life [Psalm 26].

How different is the Christian from the stoic! The latter tries to steel himself against grief by so disciplining his mind that it becomes apathetic. But discipline can accomplish only so much, and then it breaks down. Grief rushes through the slightest crack in discipline, widens it quickly, and then drowns the soul with sorrow. The stoic, knowing this, has a key card to play: suicide. This is the last, unhappy word on happiness from the stoic: to kill oneself when misery becomes too great.

Completely different is the Christian attitude toward the undeniably great evils of earthly existence. St. Augustine may again be quoted with profit:

> As we are saved, so are we blessed by hope; and as we have no hold on our safety, no more have we of our felicity, but by hope, patiently awaiting it; and being as yet in a desert of thorny dangers, all these we must constantly endure until we come to the paradise of ineffable delights, having then passed all the perils of encumbrance. This security in the life to come is the beatitude we speak of, which the philosophers, not beholding, will not believe, but forge themselves an imaginary bliss here, wherein the more their virtue assumes to itself, the falser it proves to the judgment of all others.

All Christians, so long as they truly believe in Christ, have the real possibility of being consoled and strengthened by hope. This hope, founded on the perfectly credible promises of Christ, allows

the Christians to experience even natural joys with far more enthusiasm and far less artificially imposed reserve. A great love
(which life may give a man) rejoices him beyond words to tell but
simultaneously, carries the threat that it will end with the death of
one or both lovers. The natural man, then, must see tragedy inevitably tied to his love. He must try, in one way or another, to mitigate
the impending tragedy. And how does one do this, except by holding back the fullness of his love?

The Christian can afford to love from his very depths. For he
enjoys the firm conviction that his earthly love, if only it be founded
in Christ, within the framework of Christ, will not be forever cut
down with death but will achieve perfectly in eternity what on earth
it always aspired to. For the Christian, there is no mockery in love;
there is no sweet promise, cruelly denied. For the Christian alone,
earthly love can be what every lover wants it to be: secure, serene,
perfect, undamaged by death—because it is rooted in the eternal
Person of God.

A final joy that is reserved only to the Christian remains to be
mentioned: the happiness that comes when a man discovers Christ
as the perfect Beloved. All the goodness of the universe, all the
beauty that shines forth from any created beloved, is to be found in
Christ as in the "pure exemplar," the ultimate source and principle
of all created perfections. Even more, the infinite holiness of God
shines forth from Christ. Christ is seen as the most desirable and
lovable of beings. Even to know Christ, therefore, even to dwell on
his perfections in reverent contemplation, is to sup at the perfect
banquet. Of course, as we have seen, a great effort of concentration
and recollection is needed because the values of the banquet are not
immediately present. Nonetheless, when the effort is successful,
the spirit sups at a table of unlimited splendors. Then to feel love
surging toward Christ, to respond actively with love for the Beautiful One—this is to enjoy love of a depth and height never before
imagined. Finally, to know that the love is requited—sometimes
even to *experience* the love of Christ for us—is to achieve a new
dimension of earthly bliss.

Not all believers in Christ avail themselves of the chance to experience these three climaxes of happiness that are possible with

Christ, namely, the banquet happiness of knowing him, the joy of loving him, and the new joy of knowing that the love is requited by him. Each of the faithful, however, is urged and exhorted to begin at least to learn about Christ so as to know him. And always, somewhere in the Church, a man or woman or child is to be found who has gone far beyond knowledge, who has fallen in love with Christ. This person, this *saint*, is afire with love for Christ. The love goes from the saint to Christ and then joins itself with Christ's love for man. So now, *with Christ*, the saint loves his fellow men.

Of different beginnings and backgrounds, different talents and education, different natural characteristics, all the thousands of saints agree on two basic features. Each has become like unto Christ in his moral life and each has fallen in love with Christ with "his whole heart and strength, his whole mind and soul." Each, therefore, speaks in his own way and in his own words of his delight in loving Christ, of his being enraptured by Christ, of his preferring Christ to anything else.

> For better is one day in Thy courts above thousands
> [Psalm 83:11].

For those who are blind to even natural love, for those, moreover, who appreciate natural love but sneer at the thought of a creature's loving his Creator, the saints' words about their rapture and bliss seem like romantic poetry, or even like neurotic wishful thinking. But for those who have followed us thus far, it is clear that even natural love, yielding (as it does) three climaxes of happiness, is enough to move a lover to speak of the tenderness and warmth of his love, of the soaring delight he experiences in the presence of the beloved, and of the joy beyond words when the beloved returns love for love and caresses the lover. How much greater, then, can be love for the perfect Beloved! When this love appears in a saint, only the self-blinded and the prejudiced can ignore it, or—worse—misunderstand and distort it, and only those who hate moral goodness and God can hate it. All the rest, sinner and even unbeliever though they may be, gather around the mystery of a human soul aflame with love for God and, through God, for neighbor.

The saints alone have tasted the joys of loving God. By their words, they try to lead their still unloving brethren to a greater knowledge, and then to love of God. "O taste and see that the Lord is sweet!" exhorts the Psalmist. Once the Christian has experienced this joy of loving the perfect Beloved, he understands the genuine happiness of the saints, their unconditional loyalty to Christ, for they have achieved the last insight and experience that are possible to man on earth. They have seen the overwhelming beauty and splendor of Christ. Humbly they adore Christ, boldly they love him. Embraced by him, they cannot contain their joy, which persists even in the midst of earthly evils.

> Who then shall separate us from the love of Christ? Shall tribulation? or distress? or famine? or nakedness? or danger? or persecution? or the sword?
>
> But in all these things we overcome, because of Him that hath loved us.
>
> For I am sure that neither death, nor life, nor angels, nor principalities, nor powers, nor things present, nor things to come, nor might,
>
> Nor height, nor depth, nor any other creature, shall be able to separate us from the love of God, which is in Christ Jesus our Lord.
>
> Romans 8:35, 37–39